# RON REICH

Ron Reich, by example, set the standards in levels of performance for competing individuals and teams. As an individual, he dominated competition in Ballet and Precision during the years 1987, 1988 and 1989. His peers voted him **"Most Outstanding Flyer of the Year,"** in a survey conducted by **American Kite Magazine** during **1988** and **1989**. He led his team, The Flight Squadron, to become the first WORLD CHAMPIONS in 1990. He was also the first individual to fly 3 independently controlled kites in competition. Just for the fun of it, he even flew a kite under water while on a scuba dive. Ron's main objective as a kite performer is to create an emotional feeling in the spectator. Ron Reich's performances have left many spectators with a lump in their throat and a tear in their eye.

# KITE

# *Precision*

Your Comprehensive Guide for
Flying Controllable Kites

## By Ron Reich

TUTOR TEXT®
Ramona, California

# KITE *Precision*

## Your Comprehensive Guide for Flying Controllable Kites

# By Ron Reich

Published by: **TUTOR TEXT**®
Post Office Box 1605
Ramona, CA 92065-0895

Copyright © 1993 by Ron Reich
First Printing 1993
Printed in the United States of America

Library of Congress Catalog Card Number: 93-61552

ISBN 0-9639010-2-8: $14.95 Softcover

Cover design by Cassie Reich, Graphic Designer

FLEXIFOIL® is a registered trademark of Flexifoil International.

REVOLUTION® is a registered trademark of Revolution Enterprises Incorporated.

# Table of Contents

# ACKNOWLEDGEMENTS

I want to thank all of the people around the world that have been a part of my growth as a kitest. Each individual has made a contribution to my knowledge that has led to the production of this book. This also includes the many spectators who have shown their encouragement and support by displaying their appreciation for my performances. You know who you are, and be assured that I am thankful that you have been there.

I give special thanks to the following, for their direct support in the production of this book:

Jim, Joe, and Dave Hadzicki, at **Revolution Kites** for their encouragement and the kite equipment that they provided for the photos used in the "Revolution Kite" section of this book.

Ray and Jeanne Merry, at **Cobra Kites** for their encouragement and the technical information about the "Flexifoil Kite."

Stan Swanson, at **Condor Kites** for his encouragement and the "Griffin Kite" used for photos in this book.

Nina Haddock Ph.D., M.Ed., at the Ramona Learning Center for her literary guidance throughout this book.

Cassie Reich, Graphic Designer, for the beautiful cover design.

# DEDICATION

I would like you to meet my wife, Judy. She is totally responsible for the publication of this book. She remained a dedicated supporter to my objectives as a competitive stunt kite pilot for over seven years. I always talked about writing a book to share the knowledge that I had gained. One day she asked me, "Are you serious, or are you just dreaming?" I could tell from the look in her eye that I should be sure of my answer. When I answered in the affirmative, she took control of the effort. She did all of the organization for registration and marketing. All she would let me do is write. It is because of her devoted love and support of my objectives that I dedicate this book entirely to her. This has truly been a labor of Love.

# INTRODUCTION

This is a book about how to fly controllable kites. It includes information that is helpful to Beginner, Intermediate and Advanced flyers.

The Beginning flyer will learn how to set the kite up for that first flight. The information is presented in a manner that will move the beginner into the intermediate class rapidly.

The Intermediate flyer will learn alternative methods of execution, to create different effects in a turn. Some interesting stunts are presented to challenge the intermediate flyer.

The Advanced flyer will learn to organize fundamental maneuvers into a choreographed routine. The section on flying multiple kites is a challenge for the advanced flyer.

The routines in the back of this book will be of interest to individual flyers as well as teams. The individual can select the path of a particular kite and fly its entire pattern.

This book is designed to help the reader learn the basics, and advance to the more creative aspects of flying as quickly as possible.

*Fly Safe*
*Fly for Fun*


*Ron Reich*

# *1* SETTING UP
# TO FLY

You will find it easier to handle and set up your kite if you keep your back to the wind. Also, work with the nose of the kite toward your body. A good rule of thumb is to always keep the nose of the kite into the wind.

After you have assembled your kite, hold it by the bridle lines and let the wind elevate it so that you can check it for proper assembly.

Develop a check system for your kite. I use a 5 point system to check each side of my kites.

1. Bridle outhaul connection.
2. Bridle top leg connection.
3. Bridle center connection.
4. Fly Line attachment point.
5. Sail Positioner.

Lay your lines out and stake your handles to the ground. You could lean your kite against something convenient like a trash can or a fence.

It is very important that you lean the kite back about 30 degrees when you have the handles staked. Otherwise, the kite can self-launch before you are ready.

If I did not have my hand above the nose of this kite, it would self-launch. Be sure to lean the kite back about 30 degrees whenever the handles are staked to the ground.

# DELTA KITE PARTS

| 1 | Nose |
|---|---|
| 2 | Top Spreader Spar |
| 3 | Top Spreader to Leading Edge Connector |
| 4 | Top Leg of Bridle |
| 5 | Leading Edge |
| 6 | Tow Point |
| 7 | Bridle Out-Haul |
| 8 | Bottom Spreader to Leading Edge Connector |
| 9 | Wing Tip |
| 10 | Trailing Edge |
| 11 | Bottom Spreader |
| 12 | Fly Line |
| 13 | Sail Positioner |
| 14 | Bottom Leg of Bridle |
| 15 | Bottom Tip of Center Spine |
| 16 | Bottom Spreaders to Center Spine Connector |
| 17 | Center Spine |
| 18 | Sail |

This kite is a "Griffin," made by Condor Kites. However, most Delta kites have similar parts.

# 2 POSTURE

Sport Kiting requires a certain amount of physical fitness. The effort can be reduced if you use good posture. Your posture will be somewhat dictated by the force of the wind.

For light wind, stand relaxed with one foot slightly ahead of the other. Let your arms move in harmony with the pull of the kite. Think of your arms as elastic springs keeping tension on the fly lines. Steer the kite with a gentle pulling and releasing action.

Let your arms extend forward. Your elbows should be slightly bent.

For best results, keep your hands below your shoulders.

Your hands should be 3 to 10 inches apart. This will help you maintain a reference for steering the kite.

Place one foot ahead of the other.

Some people wear cleated shoes for more traction.

It is very *important* to keep your hands between your body and the kite; otherwise, you may experience *back* and *muscle strain*.

You will soon realize that the kite pulls more in the center area of the wind window. With experience, you will learn to anticipate this area and start leaning back before the kite gets there.

# STRONG WIND FLYING

In really strong wind, if you are determined to fly, you should consider sitting on soft ground.  Spread your feet and dig in your heals.   Keep your back straight, keep your hands between your body and the kite, and lean back.   Make sure the ground behind you is soft; if a line breaks, you are going to lie down ... REAL FAST.

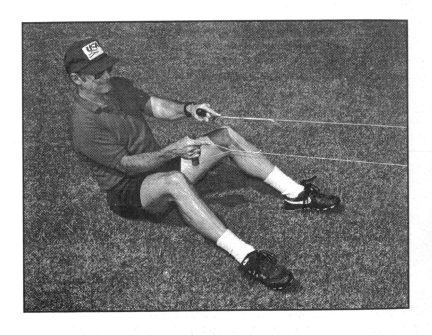

# 3 SAFETY

Safety is a serious issue. You can be seriously injured, and you can seriously injure other people with your kite. Common sense is the best defense. Apply the following fundamental rules of safety.

## FOR YOUR OWN SAFETY

**Never Allow A Kite Or Its Strings To Touch Power Lines.** Most power lines carry over 12,000 volts of electricity that can light you up, like a light bulb... ONCE !

**Never Fly A Kite During An Electrical Storm.** Ben Franklin was lucky he was only holding one string. The completed electrical circuit of holding two strings goes right through your heart. The shock could be deadly.

**Never Fly A Kite At People or Animals.** Most people do not see the humor in being scared by a kite and may respond in a manner hazardous to your health. Most kite chasing dogs love to shred kites.

**Always Stand On Solid Ground.** Loose gravel and wet grass do not provide proper traction for the power generated by kites. All the ground around your flying area should be free of obstacles: kite bags, lawn chairs and anything else you might trip over.

**Always Stay At Least 20 feet Down Wind From Any Sidewalk Or Bike Path.** When you experience a sudden drop in line tension, the natural response is to back up quickly. Most park sidewalks attract bicyclists, skaters, skate boarders, and pedestrians.

## FOR THE SAFETY OF OTHERS

**Never Fly A Kite Near An Airport.** It is against the LAW. Check with the local airport authority for the maximum authorized range and altitude for kite flying in the area. It might help to let them know you are flying kites at a fixed length of line that never exceeds 150 feet.

**Never Fly A Kite Over Or Near A Roadway.** If a motorist has had an accident, because he was distracted by your kite, you could be held liable. Your defense is pretty weak if your kite was flown over the roadway. Somebody might get hurt.

**Never Fly A Kite Over A Sidewalk Or Bike Path.** This is perhaps the most dangerous situation of all. The strings of the kite can cut a person's neck, just like the wire of a cheese cutter. You should always be on the down wind  side of the sidewalk.


\*\*\*\*\*\*\*\*\*\*
**THE SAFETY OF THE SPECTATOR IS THE RESPONSIBILITY OF THE KITE FLYER.**
\*\*\*\*\*\*\*\*\*\*

# 4 STRAIGHT LINE FLIGHT

**STRAIGHT LINE FLIGHT** is the most important primary skill you can learn for flying controllable kites.

**Horizontal** straight lines are used for ground passes.

**Vertical** straight lines are used to check fly line lengths.

Combinations of straight lines in a variety of directions are used to create geometric figures.

The general position of the hands for straight line flight is side by side. There is no absolute position for the hands during straight line flight. When the kite is on a horizontal path, you will need to compensate for the effects of gravity. Gravity will try to pull the kite to the ground; so, you must steer the kite at a slight up-angle. This angle is almost undetectable. When the kite is on a vertical path, you will need to compensate for the effects of the wind. The wind will try to push the kite toward the center of the wind window; so, you must compensate by steering at a slight angle into the wind. This angle will be more noticeable as the kite moves closer to the edge of the wind window. Any small difference in the lengths of the two fly lines will affect the position of the hands during straight line flight. As a matter of fact, the only place where the hands will be precisely side by side, assuming that the fly lines are equal length, will be straight down wind on a vertical path.

Lets practice flying horizontal passes. Fly the horizontal path as far as you can to each side of the wind window before turning to go in the other direction.

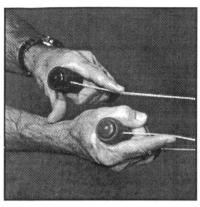

Place your hands close together. When flying your kite from right to left, keep your right thumb in contact with your left hand, wrist, or arm as a reference. When flying from left to right, use your left thumb as a reference. This will help you make the small adjustments necessary for straight line flight.

Other steering can be done by adjusting the amount of pressure that you apply to the lines with your index fingers.

Concentrate on making the kite go in a straight line. After you achieve straight line flight, start working the kite closer and closer to the ground. Your initial goal will be to fly parallel to the ground, about 4 to 8 feet above the ground. Ultimately, you will be able to fly at a consistent 1 inch above the ground from one side of the wind window to the other.

## USING STRAIGHT LINE FLIGHT TO
## TEST FOR EQUAL LENGTH FLY LINES.

Now that you can fly your kite in a straight line, lets use that ability to determine if your fly lines are equal in length. Fly the kite close to the ground. When it is just about to the center of the wind window, turn it straight up. Keep your hands close together.

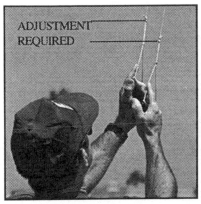

When the kite is flying straight up in the center of the wind window, **PRESS YOUR HANDS TOGETHER** tightly. This should be done when the kite is between 1/2 and 3/4 of the way up, and when the kite is still pulling. For best results the pull should be moderate. Do not wait until the kite reaches the top, because if the kite was not in the center of the wind window, it will start to turn. The kite will continue to go up to the top and hover. Examine the relative position of your hands to determine which fly line is longer. Do this test several times until the error is consistent. Then, land the kite and make the appropriate adjustment to the length of the longer fly line. Now, with the fly lines at equal length, you should find that controlling the kite is easier and more uniform.

# WIND WINDOW

THE WIND WINDOW IS A HALF HEMISPHERE

TOP

LEFT EDGE

RIGHT EDGE

POWER ZONE

EASY LANDING

BODY ZONE

EASY LANDING

LEFT

RIGHT

     The Wind Window includes the down wind area of the sky from ground level on your left up over the top of your head and down to the ground level on your right. The surface of the Wind Window is a Half Hemisphere with a radius equal to the length of your fly lines. The kite will produce the most pull, when it is in the Power Zone. The least amount of pull will be, when the kite is at the edges and the top of the wind window. Landing is easiest at the edges.

# 5 BASIC LAUNCHING AND LANDING

Place your hand on top of the handles as you remove the ground stake. This will insure that the kite does not accidentally launch. Watch the kite as you pick up your handles. Do not allow it to lean forward or it might launch before you are ready.

When you are ready to launch the kite, extend your arms toward the kite. Place one foot back in preparation for taking a few quick steps backwards. Tug both lines back past your hips as you take a few quick steps backwards. As the kite lifts into the sky, return your hands to a position in front of your body.

When you are ready to land, maneuver the kite to the edge of the wind window. Continue to point the kite into the wind as you alternate pulling and pushing gently on the bottom line to work the kite toward the ground. When the kite is about 3 feet above the ground, PUSH on the BOTTOM LINE and step quickly toward the kite. When the trailing edge is parallel to the ground, push on the other line to stop the rotation of the kite.

Different types of launches and landings are presented in other sections of this book.

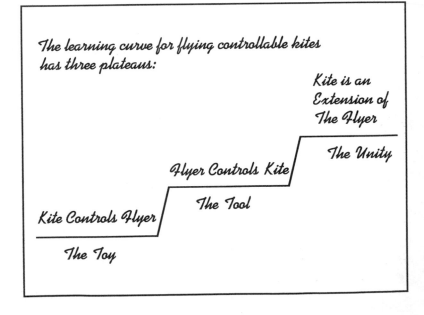

The learning curve for flying controllable kites
has three plateaus:

Kite is an
Extension of
The Flyer

The Unity

Flyer Controls Kite

The Tool

Kite Controls Flyer

The Toy

# 6 THE 4 FUNDAMENTAL TURNS

By learning these **FOUR FUNDAMENTAL TYPES OF TURNS,** you will develop a solid foundation for flying controllable kites. These turns utilize the four combinations of push and pull. Mastering these four techniques will enhance your ability to demonstrate a variety of styles. The subtle differences will be best illustrated if you practice making these turns while the kite is on a horizontal path. Your initial execution should cause the kite to turn up. After you are comfortable with the turns in an upward direction, execute each of the four types of turns in a downward direction. Whether you pull on the left line or push on the right line the kite will turn to the left; however, the action of the kite will be slightly different.

The first two turns will start with both hands extended in front of the body.  Fly the kite on a horizontal path about 20 feet above the ground.

| **PULL TO START THE TURN.** | **PUSH TO STOP THE TURN.** |
|:---:|:---:|

This type of turn is used when flying geometric figures.    It produces the smoothest turning characteristics of the kite.

| **PULL TO START THE TURN.** | **PULL OTHER HAND TO STOP THE TURN.** |
|:---:|:---:|

 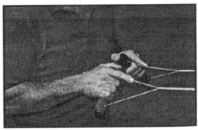

This type of turn is used to maintain the power and speed of the kite.

The last two turns will start with both hands pulled in near the chest. Fly the kite on a horizontal path about 20 feet above the ground.

### PUSH TO START THE TURN.    PULL TO STOP THE TURN.

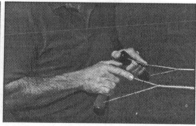

Use this turn to execute sharp corners and to snap the kite back to its original line of flight.

### PUSH TO START THE TURN.    PUSH OTHER HAND TO STOP THE TURN.

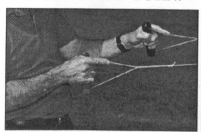

This type of turn is used to land the kite. It is also used to stall the kite in mid-air.

These 4 fundamental turns change the wind pressure on the sail of the kite.  Whenever, you add pressure to one side of the kite by pulling on it, that side of the kite speeds up. Similarly, whenever you remove pressure from one side of the kite by pushing on it, that side of the kite slows down. You do not need to understand the aerodynamics of what is happening to the kite, in order to utilize the effects created by these 4 fundamental turns.   Just realize that there are differences and apply them as needed.

## REVIEW

The **PULL/PUSH**  turn is executed with one hand, while holding the other hand stationary.  The kite will power into the turn and ease out of the turn.

The **PULL/PULL**  turn is executed first by pulling with one hand and then pulling with the other hand.  The kite will power into the turn and then maintain that power coming out of the turn.  Anytime you pull on the kite, you will add power and speed to the kite.

The **PUSH/PULL**  turn is perhaps the most versatile. Use it when you want to make sharp corners on a square or octagon.  Use it when you want to loft into a turn, and then snap the kite back on track at the end of the turn.  Use it when the kite is at the edge of the wind window and you want to turn down.  Use it at the bottom of a dive, when you want to pull out of the dive at the very last moment.

The **PUSH/PUSH**  turn is essential for landing the kite.  The objective of this turn is to remove the power from the kite and usually includes walking or running toward the kite.  You will also find this turn useful for initiating a side slide motion of the kite.  Fly the kite toward the edge of the wind window about 40 feet above the ground.  Push on the top wing.  This will start the kite's turning downward toward the ground.  Let the nose of the kite come around and then just as it starts to point straight up, push the other hand forward to stop the turning.  Steady the kite with the nose up and slide it sideways.

# 7 SPEED CONTROL

I'd have to say that speed control has made the most significant contribution to my success.  This control demonstrates the ability to take command over the effects of the wind on the kite.

The technique of speed control is centered around monitoring and adjusting the tension in the fly lines.  The speed of the kite is directly proportional to the tension in the fly lines.

**MORE  TENSION  PRODUCES  FASTER  SPEED.**

**LESS  TENSION  PRODUCES  SLOWER  SPEED.**

The amount of pressure that the handles are exerting on your hands is a direct indication of the amount of tension in the fly lines.  Place your index fingers on the lines in order to provide a sensitive method of monitoring the tension.

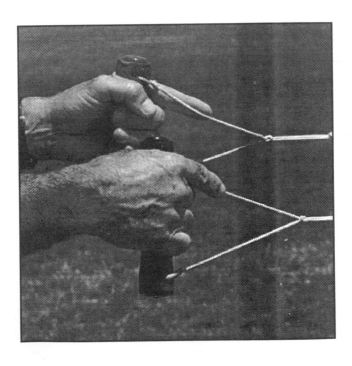

As the kite moves through the wind window, the amount of pull it exerts will change. To demonstrate this to yourself, stand stationary and fly your kite from one extreme edge of the wind window to the other, concentrate on the amount of tension you feel in the fly lines. If you do not do anything to compensate for the change in tension, the kite will naturally change speed as it moves across the wind window.

To demonstrate that you are in control of the speed of the kite, you will need to move forward and backward. Some control can be accomplished by just moving your arms. The really fine control is accomplished by rotating the wrists and applying pressure on the fly line with the index finger.

# CONSTANT  TENSION

# EQUALS

# CONSTANT  SPEED

When the kite moves at a constant speed through a geometric figure it appears to be a machine on a guided track. That appearance should be one of the primary objectives of the flyer when executing compulsory figures in competition.

Speed control is also very important when flying to music. The speed of the kite and the changes in the speed of the kite, are used to reflect the mood and the changes in the mood of the music. I suggest that you spend a lot of time working with the control of the tension in the fly lines. Be sensitive to what you feel. You may find that you can feel the slightest flutter of the trailing edge of the kite. The use of lighter fly line and handles will increase your sensitivity. Really light fly line, such as 50 pound test, is not recommended for competition. But, it can be used to increase your awareness of the vibrations that are taking place at the kite. Sometimes, when the fly line is pulled really tight, it will start singing to you. The lighter the fly line, the lighter the handles should be. In wind less than 3 mph, some top flyers fly their kites without handles. They put a loop of heavy sleeving on the end of their 20 to 50 pound test lines.

# $8$ LEADING EDGE LAUNCH

The ability to launch the kite from this position is perhaps the most useful skill you can learn. When you are proficient at this launch you will only need to walk out to your kite to set it up, when it is lying flat on the ground with the nose pointing toward you.

OPTIONAL

Leading edge launches are easier if the bridle tow point is moved toward the nose of the kite. Temporarily move it 1/4 to 1/2 inch toward the nose. Mark the original position before you change it. Be sure to put it back when you are finished practicing the leading edge launch.

Practice the leading edge launch when the kite is positioned near the edge of the wind window. Point the kite heading into the wind.

While keeping a slight amount of tension in the line attached to the leading edge on the ground, pull gently on the wing that is in the air until the tip is tilting toward you about 30 degrees.

Start backing up slowly. Keep some tension on the ground line as you increase the amount of pull on the wing in the air. The kite should start to slide into the wind. Increase the speed you are backing up and the nose should begin to lift off the ground.

Continue to increase the speed  you are backing up and the kite will lift into the air.

## COMMON ERRORS

When attempting the leading edge launch, the most common error is not keeping enough tension on the ground line. This causes the kite to flip over, putting the other leading edge on the ground. Another common error is to pull too hard on the wing in the air as the kite is coming off the ground. This causes the kite to overturn, collapse, and come back to the ground.

## LEADING EDGE LANDING

The leading edge landing should only be done on a soft surface and in winds less than 5 mph.

Start with the kite in the upper right hand corner of the wind window.  Fly the kite on a path toward the ground, to the left side of the wind window, keeping the bottom leading edge parallel to the ground.  An instant before the left leading edge makes contact with the ground, quickly push the right hand forward about 2 feet.

The object is to give the appearance that the kite has been stuck in the mud.  When done correctly, the kite should stop all motion instantly.  There should be no bounce or rocking motion.  The instant stop will indicate that the flyer has flown the kite into the ground intentionally and that it has not been a crash landing.

From this position, the kite is now ready for the Leading Edge Launch.

# 9 TIP STAND

To execute a tip stand, position the kite on the ground straight down wind.   Set it with the right tip about a foot closer to you than the left tip.   Let the kite lean back about 20 degrees.

Gently pull on the right line.   When the left wing tip starts to lift off of the ground, stop pulling and use the left line to steady the kite.  If you pull too much on the right wing, the entire kite will rise off of the ground.

While balancing the kite on its right tip, carefully step toward the kite. If the tip has enough grip on the ground, you can let the kite lay quite far back. Soft sand works very well.

## WALKING THE KITE

Walking the kite uses the same technique as the tip stand. The difference is that when the left wing starts to lift off of the ground, you pull on the left line as you release the tension on the right line. The kite will assume a new position on the ground where by the left wing tip is now closer to you than the right tip. Now start to execute a left tip stand by gently pulling on the left wing. As the right wing starts to lift off of the ground, pull on the right line as you release the tension on the left line. The kite will now be positioned back on the ground with the right wing tip closer to you. You must also take steps backwards to compensate for the kite's walking toward you. You will find the execution is easier if you start with the left line completely slack as you gently pull on the right line and make the right line completely slack when you pull on the left line.

# TIP DRAG

Dragging one of the tips of the kite along the ground during a ground pass is easiest, when the kite is headed into the wind and toward the edge of the wind window. The hand holding the line attached to the wing on the ground should be held stationary while the adjustements are made with the other hand.

# *10* NOSE DOWN LAUNCH

Position the kite straight down wind, nose down. Pull gently on both lines and balance the kite on its nose with both tips at equal distance off the ground. You should observe and take note that the right side of the kite is on your left and that the left side of the kite is on your right.

Pull gently on the left line and push on the right line. The left leading edge will go to the ground.

This picture shows the left tip of the kite about 10 inches off the ground.

Pull gently on the right line and push on the left line. The right leading edge will go to the ground.

This picture shows the right tip of the kite about 10 inches off the ground.

Start rocking the kite back and forth by alternately pushing and pulling the right and left lines. This launch is going to take advantage of the momentum that the kite develops during the rocking motion. Apply the following process to launch the kite.

First, decide which direction you want to launch the kite. If you are going to launch to your right, then you will give a strong tug on the left line. If you are going to launch to your left, then you will give a strong tug on the right line.

Second, observe and take note of the precise moment that the kite's leading edge tips are about 10 inches off the ground. This will be the precise moment that you will give a strong tug on the appropriate line to launch the kite.

Third, launch the kite with a strong tug when the wing tip is headed toward the ground and is passing through the point about 10 inches above the ground. The faster the rocking action, the easier this launch will be.

## COMMON MISTAKES

Trying to launch with very little or no rocking action will just flip the kite over to the other leading edge on the ground.

It will be difficult trying to develop a uniform rocking motion when the kite is near the edge of the wind window.

# TURTLE LAUNCH

Note: This launch requires the kite to be outfitted with sail positioners.

Position the kite about 50 feet in from the right edge of the wind window, with the kite on its back, and the nose pointing into the wind.

"Looks like a turtle to me."

Pull on the left line causing the kite to rotate the left tip into the wind. The kite should stay flat on the ground. As the kite rotates around, the wind will go under the left leading edge and flip the kite over onto its face, bridle side down.

The trick is to pull on the right line as the left tip is passing through 12 o'clock high. It is important that the wind be the force that has raised the left leading edge off the ground and not the fact that you are pulling on the left line. Also, the tip must be moving and not stalled out in the vertical position.

When done properly, the wind will catch under the face of the kite before it gets to the ground, and lift it into the sky.

# 11 WRAPPED FLIP LAUNCH

## CAUTION !

## THIS STUNT COULD TEAR YOUR KITE

### Use an old kite to learn this stunt.

Here is a novel stunt for you to try in winds of about 5 mph. A nose prop will be required.

## PREPARATION

Remove all twists from the pair of fly lines.

Position the kite on the ground in the center of the wind window.

Lay the kite face down on top of the fly lines with the nose pointing into the wind (toward the handles).

Position yourself on the down wind (trailing edge) side of the kite.

Very carefully roll the kite on the fly lines.

Raise the trailing edge of the kite, leaving the nose on the ground.

Lay the kite on its back with the nose now pointing toward you. Raise the nose of the kite leaving the trailing edge on the ground.

Lay the kite back on its face with the nose pointing toward the handles.

Examine the location of the fly lines as they wrap around the kite.   At the trailing edge, the lines should be between the sail standoffs and the center spine.   At the leading edge, the fly lines should be above the top spreader vinyl connectors.

Prop the nose of the kite up off the ground about 8 to 10 inches.  Do not stick the prop into the ground.  It needs to be loose so that it can fall flat during the launch.

Give a firm steady pull on the fly lines, while taking a few steps backwards.  The kite will unwind from the fly lines as it leaves the ground and display a very entertaining back flip launch.  The firm pull should NOT be a hard jerk.   With some practice, you can add more wraps and do double and even triple back flips in the take-off.

## CAUTION !
## THE FLY LINE COULD CUT YOUR KITE.
## BE SURE TO USE AN OLD KITE.

# PASTING

Find a smooth metal pole down wind from a satisfactory flying area. Make sure that the pole does NOT have any signs attached to it. On a day when the wind is blowing at a nice steady 5 miles per hour, try pasting your kite onto the pole. The pasting is accomplished by executing basic landing techniques. First, lean your kite against the base of the pole and stretch out your fly lines. Place a marker on the ground about 5 feet further away than your handles. Stand about 10 feet behind the marker to fly your kite. Fly a ground pass toward the pole. Walk in to slow the kite down. Time the landing execution such that when the center spine is vertical, it is also lined up with the pole. Step toward the kite and allow the wind to press the kite against the pole. Resume flying by pulling on both lines.

# *12* **FLYING THE SHADOW**

The next time you are on the field with your kite, take notice of where the sun is. If you are lucky, the sun will be somewhere about mid-sky and straight down wind from you. If you were to fly your kite normally, you would be looking straight into the sun. Look for the shadow of the kite on the ground. When the kite is below the sun, the shadow will be in front of you. When the kite is above the sun, the shadow will be behind you. Shadow flying is easiest to learn when the sun is near the top of the wind window. The kite will need to fly easily above the sun. Fly the kite on a ground pass to a position below the sun. Then, turn the kite to go straight up at the sun. Notice that the shadow of the kite is coming straight toward you. As the shadow passes by you, raise your hands over your head and turn your body to the same side as the shadow. Keep your eyes on the shadow.

One word of caution. Be aware that the fly lines are passing by your head. Be careful not to let the line catch on your ears or glasses.

The control of the kite is actually quite simple. The best learning action is to alternate pushing right and left, causing the kite's shadow to weave back and forth in front of you.

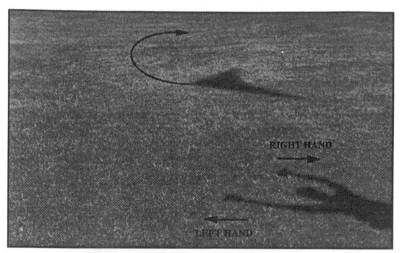

To turn the shadow clockwise, push the left hand into the wind and pull the right hand toward your body.

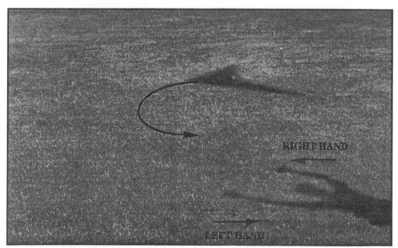

To turn the shadow counterclockwise, push the right hand into the wind, and pull the left hand toward your body.

## CAUTION !!   CAUTION !! CAUTION   !!

DO NOT ATTEMPT THIS ON A CROWDED FIELD.

DO NOT ATTEMPT THIS IN WINDS GREATER THAN 10 mph.

Your back is to the kite.    Therefore, you will undoubtedly lose control the first few times you try it.

Once you get the hang of it, try to maneuver the shadow to hover near where you are standing, so that you can step on it.  Spectators standing up wind will soon get the idea of what you are doing and be entertained by any antics that you can do with the shadow.

# *13* DOG-STAKE FLYING

Dog-Stake flying presents a unique opportunity for you to directly interrelate with your kite. A cork screw dog stake is anchored securely into the ground to serve as a pulley. The fly lines are laced through the open loop at the top of the dog stake. The flyer will stand next to the kite and the fly lines will go from the flyer upwind to the dog stake and back to the kite.

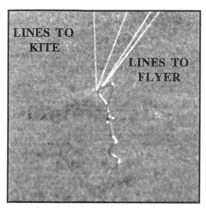

LINES TO KITE

LINES TO FLYER

Screw the dog stake at least 6 inches into the ground. Pull up on it to make sure that it is secure.

NOTE: It is a good idea to examine the inside of the loop at the top of the dog stake, and remove any metal burrs that could damage your fly lines. The inside corners should be very smooth. Use at least 200 lb. test fly line.

Locate the right edge of the wind window and land your kite there. Set the handles down and install the dog stake halfway between your handles and the kite. The opening in the eye of the dog stake should be on the up wind side. Place the fly lines on the down wind side of the dog stake. Get the handles and bring them back with you to the dog stake. Make sure you know which are the right and left handles. Stand on the up wind side of the dog stake. Grasp the lines coming from the kite. Bend the lines halfway around and through the eye of the dog stake. Caution, do not make a complete wrap around the dog stake. Now, take your handles to the kite. Place the right and left handles into the right and left hands.

Don't reverse them. Assume the position shown in the photo. When you launch your kite from this position, give a little extra pull with the left hand. This will cause the kite to come up and turn away from you. When the kite is flying away from you, pull on the right hand to cause the kite to turn up. Most of your pulling, pushing, and walking will be toward the dog stake rather than toward your kite.

When the kite is coming toward you, pull on the left line to cause the kite to turn up. As you look at this photo, you will notice that the left wing is up. I still remind myself that I need to pull left to turn the kite up when it is coming toward me.

Prepare for the "Catch" by moving about 15 feet further away from the dog stake than the kite. When the kite is coming toward you, slow it down by walking toward the dog stake. With practice, you will learn the walking speed and distance necessary to make an easy catch. When you want to resume flying, release the kite as you take a few steps backwards and pull on the left line to turn the kite up and away from you.

As you walk backwards away from the dog stake, you will notice a significant difference in the amount of pull. This is due to the angle of the lines that are bent around the dog stake, and the amount of wind force on the kite in different positions in the wind window. To reduce the amount of wear on your lines, do most of your walking backwards when the kite is at the edge of the wind window or high in the sky.

I prefer to use 300lb. Spectra. My lines are 150 feet long. This produces a relative fly line length of 75 feet because the lines are bent in half at the dog stake.

To prepare for the "Landing Catch," move about 15 feet further away from the dog stake than the kite. Slow the kite as it approaches a position above and in front of you. As it passes, push the right hand forward and step toward the kite. When the trailing edge of the kite is parallel to the ground, push the left hand forward to stop the rotation. Continue walking toward the kite as it drifts down into your outstretched hands. With practice, you will learn the walking speed and distance necessary to make an easy catch. When you are ready to resume flying, step backwards until the lines are taut with your arms stretched forward about waist high. The nose of the kite should tilt back slightly toward the top of your head. Toss the kite straight up into the sky; in the same motion, pull both lines back over your head. Pull the left line a little more to turn the kite toward the center of the wind window.

## PRAISE THE KITE

    I call this the "Praise The Kite" flight position. When the kite is about 20 feet off the ground and coming toward you, walk toward the dog stake to slow the kite down. When you are about 15 feet closer to the dog stake than the kite, raise both hands above your head and turn to face the kite as it approaches a position on the other side of you from the dog stake. All of this is done with a fluid motion. Push the left hand toward the kite to cause it to turn up. If the kite is high enough, Push the right hand toward the kite and it will turn down. Steering will be easiest if you keep your hands raised in "Praise to The Kite."

*Flying Controllable Kites will
expand your Environmental awareness.*

# *14* MULTIPLE KITE

# CONTROL

# BE YOUR OWN TEAM

## FLY 2, 3, 4, or 5
## INDEPENDENTLY
## CONTROLLED
## KITES BY YOURSELF

I have included this section for those of you who thrive on coordination challenges. This section provides a brief introduction to the concept of flying more than one controllable kite at a time. There are a lot of people around the world who fly 2 independently controllable kites at the same time. I will show you 3 different ways to choose from. There are less than 10 people in the world who fly 3 kites at a time, and less than 5 people who have flown 4 or 5 at a time. I will show you the methods that I use for the greater numbers.

\*\*\*\*\*\*\*\*\*\*\*\*\*\*\*\*\*\*\*\*\*\*\*\*\*\*\*\*\*\*\*\*\*\*\*\*\*\*\*\*\*\*\*\*

## WARNING !!!  WARNING !!!

## THERE ARE DEFINITE PHYSICAL HAZARDS IN THESE METHODS I'M ABOUT TO SHOW YOU.  YOU ARE RESPONSIBLE FOR YOUR OWN SAFETY IF YOU ATTEMPT ANY OF THESE METHODS.

\*\*\*\*\*\*\*\*\*\*\*\*\*\*\*\*\*\*\*\*\*\*\*\*\*\*\*\*\*\*\*\*\*\*\*\*\*\*\*\*\*\*\*\*

## 3 METHODS FOR FLYING 2 KITES:

COMMON POINT

### "COMMON POINT"

I tie the left line of the right kite and the right line of the left kite, to a strong bridle centered in front of my belt buckle.  I then control the kites by pushing and pulling the outside fly lines about that common point.

The common point should be located such that when the handles are positioned for straight flight, your hands are at a comfortable distance in front of your body.

Both kites turn to the right when you pull the right line past the common point and push the left line forward of the common point.

The two kites will turn away from each other if you pull both hands back past the common point.

The two kites will turn toward each other if you push both hands forward of the common point. Be sure that the kites have enough room to turn before you do this.

If I am surprised by an excessive gust of wind, I will let go of the handles to reduce the pull.

## "HIPS AND HANDS"

Control one of the kites with your hips. Tie the right line to your right hip and tie the left line to your left hip. Let this kite fly in front of the kite that you fly with your hands. Rotate your right hip back to cause the hip kite to turn to the right . Reverse for a left turn.

Turning the two kites in opposite directions is a real body twister. To turn the hip kite to the right and the hand kite to the left, rotate the hips to the right and rotate the shoulders to the left. This method is bound to keep you slim and trim.

The **"CONTROL BAR"** method of flying two kites requires the two control lines of a single kite to be attached to opposite end of a sturdy control bar. The bar should be about 16 inches long and made of strong material. I use 3/4 inch diameter wooden dowels. The control of the kite is executed by rotating the wrist. The string from the thumb end of the handle goes to the inside wing of the kite. Steering the kites seems natural when I hold the bars with my thumbs pointing toward the inside. When I rotate the left thumb IN and the right thumb OUT, both kites turn to the right. When rotating my shoulders to the right, this hand action naturally follows. When I spread my hands apart, the thumbs go out and the kites fly apart.

### "3 KITES"

By adding the hip kite of method 2 to the two kites of method 1, you can be in control of 3 kites at the same time. I prefer a steady 5mph breeze for flying 3 kites.

When you want all 3 kites to turn to the right, pull the right hand past the common point, push the left hand forward of the common point, and rotate the hips to the right. Reverse these for a left turn.

### "5 KITES"

You can control 5 kites at the same time, if you add the control bar kites to the 3 kite method. "Riiiight" To my knowledge, there are only three of us in the World that have ever tried it. Of these, I think only 1 of us has been able to keep them aloft for more than a minute.

*No, it's not me... Yet.*

*Flying Controllable Kites is the Practical Alternative to Work.*

# 15 SELECTING A KITE

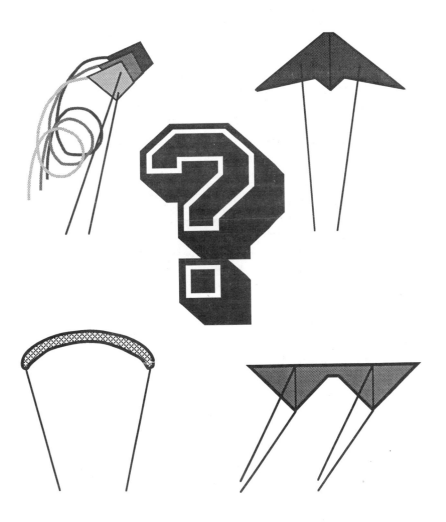

## SELECTING A KITE

Selecting your first controllable kite can be difficult. Here are some of the characteristics related to each of the 4 most popular styles.

**DIAMONDS**            **RECTANGLES**
**DELTAS**              **QUADLINED**

**DIAMONDS:** At first glance, these kites look like the kites we made in grade school. Today, these kites are available with two strings. The two strings allow you to tilt the kite while it is flying. This changes the way the wind pushes on the kite. Because of this change, you can steer the kite around in the sky. The size of the diamond kite is normally determined by the length of the center spine. Sizes range from 15 inches to over 5 feet. Most of them require at least 8 mph wind to fly. This number can be reduced to about 2mph by changing to special lightweight sticks. The diamond kites are especially pretty when several of them are hooked together in a train and dressed up with long colorful tails. The prices of the diamond kites range from $15 to over $200.

**DELTAS:** The delta kites provide the largest selection of size, color and performance characteristics. The size of a delta kite is determined by the width of its base which is referred to as its "wing span". Sizes range from 12 inches to over 15 feet. The ripstop nylon and carrington fabrics used to make these kites give them the appearance of stained glass in the sky. In general, the kites smaller than 6 ft. require at least a 6mph breeze. Most 6 ft. and larger kites can be flown in a 2 mph breeze. With special sticks and lightweight fabric, these kites can even be flown indoors with no breeze. The flyer walks backwards to create his own breeze. Over 80% of the kites flown in competition are 6 ft. and 8 ft. deltas. Some people refer to the 8 ft. delta as the standard size. The prices of the delta kites range from $20 to over $400.

**RECTANGLES:** Only a few styles of rectangular kites are available. Each size is determined by its long dimension. They are about 3 to 4 times as long as they are wide. They range in length from 4 ft. to 16 ft. Some of these kites are referred to as soft kites because they have no sticks, and they can be stuffed into a small bag for easy transport. Most rectangular kites have cells that are filled by the wind. This book has a special section devoted to the Flexifoil kite because of its reputation for power and speed. The prices of the rectangular kites range from $50 to over $300.

**QUADLINED:** This is the newest concept in controllable kites. They are in a class all their own because they are controlled with 4 strings. Since the introduction of the Revolution kite, two primary styles, *framed* and *soft*, have become available. The size of a *framed* quadlined kite is determined by the length of its width. Sizes range from 4 ft. to 9 ft. The size of a *soft* cellular quadlined kite is determined by its sail area. Sizes range from 15 sq. ft. to 50 sq. ft. All of the quadlined kites are extremely maneuverable. These kites can fly forwards, backwards, sideways, and even be stopped in mid-sky. This book has a special section devoted to the Revolution kite because of its revolutionary contribution to kiting. The prices of the quadlined kites range from $100 to over $500.

**CLOSING COMMENT:** If you are considering your first purchase, you should realize that any one of these kites will give you many hours of enjoyment. If you already own a controllable kite and are considering another one, I suggest you consider a different style. Round out your collection before you start repeating. Each of the 4 styles provides a different set of challenges.

*Learning and Sharing "is"*
*the Heartbeat of Kiting.*

# 16 FLEXIFOIL®

## INTRODUCTION

Special attention is given to the FLEXIFOIL kite because of its ability to generate speed and power. The Flexifoil has been clocked at well over 100 miles per hour. These high speeds are achieved because of the unique ram-air construction. The Flexifoil is configured with cells that inflate as the wind is passing through a screen on the leading edge. When the kite is fully inflated, it has an airfoil cross section which produces considerable lift, speed, and power.

# TOPICS COVERED IN THIS SECTION

CONSTRUCTION

LAUNCHING

BASIC CONTROL

GROUND RECOVERY

THE FLEXI-FLIP

THE FLEXI-FLOAT

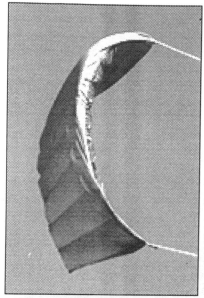

## CONSTRUCTION

The Flexifoil kite has a single spar that runs the length of the leading edge. There is no bridle. The lines tie directly onto the ends of the spar. The sail is configured with pockets separated by membranes that run from the leading edge back to the trailing edge. There is a screen across the front of the kite that allows the wind to inflate the pockets. When these pockets are inflated, the profile shape of the kite becomes an airfoil similar to an airplane's wing. In general these kites are rectangles about 3 to 4 times longer than they are wide. The normal flying configuration of the kite is to be bent in an arc. Turning is created by distorting this arc, producing an imbalance of the lift about the center of the kite. A larger distortion of the arc, will cause the kite to turn tighter.

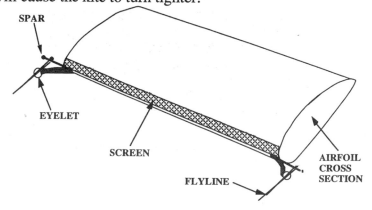

SPAR

EYELET

SCREEN

FLYLINE

AIRFOIL
CROSS
SECTION

## LAUNCHING THE FLEXIFOIL

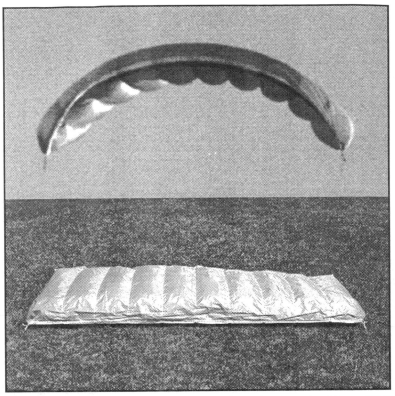

The leading edge spar needs to be bent before the kite will lift off the ground. Allow the wind to inflate the sail and then gently pull on the lines. The tips of the spar will bend and the kite will lift off the ground. As a beginner, you may need to walk slowly backwards until the kite lifts off the ground. The trailing edge of the kite will become more visible as the kite rises into the sky. The spar will bend to produce the proper flying shape. The pull will increase, so be sure to have solid footing. CAUTION, do NOT jerk on the kite during the launch. A jerk will cause the spar to reflex in the wrong direction and drive the kite back to the ground. The Flexifoil kite flies in the direction of the bend created in the leading edge spar.

## BASIC CONTROL

The Flexifoil kite provides the flyer with an opportunity to experience an aerobic exercise. The turning radius of the kite is larger than the delta shaped kites. A tight right turn is created by moving the left hand completely forward of the body and the right hand extended behind the body. This full arm motion, combined with the powerful pull of the kite is definitely an aerobic exercise. Make the transitions from right turns to left turns with a fluid motion in order to maintain the required curvature in the spar. If the spar is allowed to straighten out, then the kite will have no power. A gentle pull on both lines will reset the bend in the spar, and the kite will resume normal flight. An Ultraflex spar will make flying in low wind easier. In 2 to 5 miles per hour wind, you could use 30 to 50 foot fly lines, and fly the kite in circles around you. To fly your kite in a circle you will need to walk or run in a circle, which will add to the aerobics of your exercise.

One can create advanced maneuvers by intentionally causing the spar to become straight or reflex. See Flexi-Flip and Flexi-Float at the end of this section.

## GROUND RECOVERY

**PREPARATION:**   I recommend that you mark each of your lines with a felt tipped marker.   From your handles, measure a distance equal to the length of your kite, and put a bold mark.   For example, measure 10 feet for a 10 foot kite, and measure 8 feet for a 8 foot kite, and so on.

Now, when your Flexifoil is lying on the ground upside down, there is a fairly easy way to turn it over without walking out to the kite.   Pull gently on one of the lines until the kite is angled about 45 degrees relative to your line of sight.

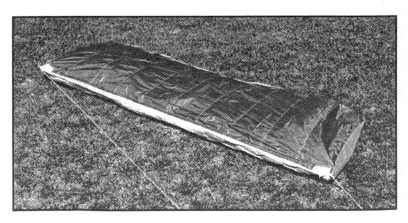

With the hand that is holding the line attached to the tip of the kite that is farthest away from you, grasp that line at the mark that is at a distance equal to the length of your kite.

Give a firm hard jerk on this line. If done correctly, the tip you have jerked will pass underneath the other line. When this happens, release the grip at the mark on the line you have jerked, and then pull gently on the other line to bring that tip forward until both lines are even. During this process, the wind will blow the sail of the kite over the top of the spar placing the kite in a position ready for launch. Whenever possible, jerk on the line underneath. CAUTION, practice this recovery technique on soft grass to reduce the possibility of damaging your kite.

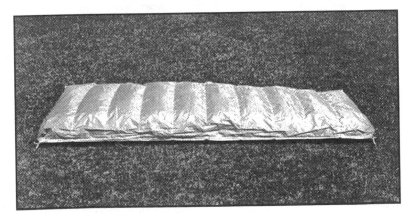

## THE FLEXI-FLIP

The Flexi-Flip stunt is unique to the Flexifoil kite. The kite can be made to flip between the fly lines, pivoting around its leading edge spar. This maneuver can be produced when the kite is flying on a vertical path headed up or down, and with experience, you can even flip it when the kite is on a horizontal path just a few feet above the ground.

Fly the kite on a vertical path headed toward the top of the wind window. As it approaches the top, place both handles into the same hand. Position the hand holding the handles as far down at your side as you can. It is important to keep this hand down low until the last step. With the free hand, reach as far up toward the kite as you can and grab both lines. Give a firm tug on both lines all the way down to the hand holding the two handles. This action accelerates the kite forward and adds extra lift to the leading edge of the kite. Immediately release the two lines and reach up toward the kite with both hands, and separate the handles back to their appropriate hands. This final action should have produced considerable slack in the lines. The reflex action of the spar will cause the sail to do a back flip over the leading edge.

## THE FLEXI-FLOAT

The Flexi-Float is a stunt that causes the Flexifoil kite to appear suspended, floating like a magic carpet in the sky. This takes advantage of the kite's need to be bent in order to fly. The bend is intentionally removed, causing the kite to float.

Fly the kite on a horizontal pass near the ground and then turn it to fly straight up in the center of the wind window. When the kite is about halfway, jerk and release both fly lines very quickly. And in conjunction with the release, start running toward the kite to cause the lines to go slack. The stroke of the jerk should be about 2 feet. Once the kite has started to float, you can maintain the float by not allowing any tension to return to the lines. When you are ready to resume normal flight take a few steps backward and pull gently on the lines. The leading edge spar will bend and you are back in business.

*Flying Controllable Kites provides the individual an opportunity to experience the effects of one of Mother Natures unpredictable elements on a man made object.*

# *17* **REVOLUTION**®

## INTRODUCTION

Specific attention is given to the Revolution kite, because of its revolutionary contribution to the whole world of kiting. Until the introduction of the Revolution kite in January of 1989, most controllable kites were limited to flying in the direction that they were pointing. The Revolution kite presented the flyer with the opportunity to maneuver the kite in any direction. For example: *forward, reverse, sideways, upside down, and even diagonally.* Not to mention the ability to *completely stop* the kite and hover it in the center of the wind window.

**The REVOLUTION® KITE
is truly REVOLUTIONARY.**

# TOPICS COVERED IN THIS SECTION

▼▼     PRINCIPLE OF DESIGN

▼▼     CONTROL TERMINOLOGY

▼▼     BASIC CONTROL

▼▼     UPRIGHT LAUNCH

▼▼     INVERTED LAUNCH

▼▼     ADVANCED CONTROL

▼▼     PUSH/PULL APPLICATIONS

▼▼     SIDE SLIDE

▼▼     SLOW MOTION  REVOLUTION

▼▼     3-D FLYING

Most of this information is covered by the free instructional video that comes with the kite.

## PRINCIPLE OF DESIGN

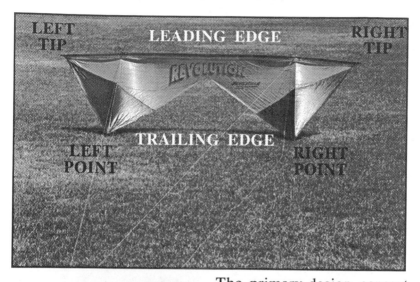

The primary design concept and flight principle of the Revolution kite allows the flyer to change the angle of attack of the kite while in flight. The shape of the kite resembles 2 separate triangles that are attached in the center. Two fly lines are attached to each triangle. This allows the flyer to tilt the triangles relative to the leading edge. If both triangles are tilted in the same direction, then the kite will fly straight in that direction. If the triangles are tilted in opposite directions, then the kite will spin like a propeller. The flyer applies a wrist rotate action for the primary steering control and a push/pull action for enhanced control.

# CONTROL TERMINOLOGY

BALANCED        FORWARD        REVERSE

RIGHT TURN        LEFT TURN

RIGHT TIP UP        LEFT TIP UP

## BASIC CONTROL

The Revolution kite is controlled with 4 fly lines. Two lines are attached to each side of the kite, one at the top and one at the bottom. A separate handle is used to control each side of the kite. The top lines from the kite are attached to the tops of the handles, and the bottom lines are attached to the bottoms of the handles. When the bottom of a handle is pointed at the kite, the leading edge of that side of the kite is tilted into the wind. When the top of a handle is pointed at the kite, the trailing edge of that side of the kite is pointed into the wind. By selectively applying tension to the lines, you can point any edge of the kite into the wind and cause the kite to fly in that direction.

The various combinations are:

TENSION APPLIED TO ---------> KITE WILL

| | |
|---|---|
| Both Tops. | Fly toward leading edge. |
| Both Bottoms. | Fly toward trailing edge. |
| Right Top, Left Bottom. | Spin Counterclockwise. |
| Left Top, Right Bottom. | Spin Clockwise. |
| Top and Bottom Right. | Slide toward right tip. |
| Top and Bottom Left. | Slide toward left tip. |

APPLY TENSION TO ------------> BY POINTING

| | |
|---|---|
| Both Tops. | Both Thumbs Back. |
| Both Bottoms. | Both Thumbs Toward Kite. |
| Right Top, Left Bottom. | Right Thumb Back and Left Thumb Toward Kite. |
| Left Top, Right Bottom. | Left Thumb Back and Right Thumb Toward Kite. |

BY EVENLY PULLING

| | |
|---|---|
| Top and Bottom Right. | Both Right Lines. |
| Top and Bottom Left. | Both Left Lines. |

## UPRIGHT LAUNCH

Let the kite lean back about 10 degrees. Point your thumbs back allowing the bottom lines to become slack. Take a couple of steps backward as you jerk the handles toward your shoulders. Keep your elbows down and near your sides. After the kite has lifted off of the ground, reposition your hands back in front of your body. Point your right thumb at the kite to turn it to the right and point your left thumb at the kite to turn it to the left. Point both thumbs at the kite to slow it down and to back it up.

## INVERTED LAUNCH

Launch the kite from the inverted position by pointing both thumbs toward the kite, and then give a firm tug on both handles at the same time. When the kite has lifted off of the ground, about 5 feet, rotate one of the thumbs back to turn the kite. When the leading edge is pointing away from the ground, point the other thumb back to fly the kite up into the sky.

## QUICK REFERENCE TUNING

I use the Inverted Launch to check the line length of the bottom lines relative to the top lines. If the kite does not lift off of the ground from the inverted position, then I shorten the bottom lines about one inch and try again. If the kite does lift off of the ground, and then one of the points flips in front of the kite, I lengthen the bottom set of fly lines by about one inch.

## IMPORTANT NOTE

Push-Pull actions are NOT required to fly the Revolution kite. In fact, beginners should make every effort to keep their elbows in contact with their sides to avoid any accidental push or pull reflex action. Learning to fly the kite will be much quicker with this technique.

## ADVANCED CONTROL

The selective simultaneous application of the wrist rotate and push-pull actions will allow the flyer to maintain elevation while the kite is spinning like a propeller. A delicate balance of all four lines will allow the flyer to maintain a stationary position in the sky, regardless of the angular orientation of the kite. A gentle balanced pull on one side of the stationary kite will cause it to slide toward that side of the kite. This sliding action can be executed regardless of the angular orientation of the kite. An advanced flyer will continually monitor the tension in each of the 4 fly lines.

## PUSH/PULL APPLICATIONS

Pushing and Pulling will shift the force of the wind to one side of the kite or the other. The application of pushing and pulling in combination with rotating the wrists will allow the flyer to proportion the amount of tension applied to each of the 4 fly lines. A resultant dominant force can be achieved in any direction relative to the kite. This force will be used to offset the effects of gravity when the kite is hovering. Selective application of the pushing and pulling will allow the flyer to create special effects in the flight of the kite.

## SIDE SLIDE

Position the kite, inverted, in the center of the wind window, on a relatively smooth surface. Freshly mowed grass is best. You should take note that the right side of the kite is now on your left, and it will be affected when you work the right handle. Keep the kite on the ground during this exercise. Point the right thumb at the kite while you gently pull the right hand back, and at the same time, push the left hand forward. The kite should start to slide toward your left. In light wind, you may need to point both of your thumbs slightly toward the kite to reduce the amount of friction that it has with the ground. Reversing the pushing and pulling will cause the kite to go in the other direction. Slide the kite back and forth until you are confident that you can apply the appropriate push and pull combination to get the kite to go in the direction you want. As you practice this, gradually start pointing your thumbs further toward the kite. The kite will start to lift off the ground. You must balance the amount of wrist rotate action to keep the kite horizontal. As you develop your skill to maintain the kite in a stationary horizontal position, the side slide will become easier.

## GROUND FLIP FROM INVERTED TO UPRIGHT

Point the Left Thumb back and the Right Thumb toward the kite. Give a sharp tug on both handles at the same time. Be sure to keep the left thumb back and the right thumb pointed toward the kite.

The left tip of the kite will stay on the ground as the right side of the kite flips over the top. After the right tip has passed over the top, rotate the left thumb toward the kite to keep the kite on the ground. Or, to launch the kite, point the right thumb back just before the right side reaches the ground.

## STABILIZING IN THE VERTICAL POSITION

Stabilizing the kite in the vertical position is easiest if one of the tips is on the ground. This is called a tip stand. The kite can be raised into a Left tip stand by pointing the Right Thumb Back and the Left Thumb Toward The Kite.

The balance is maintained by carefully adjusting the angle of the side of the kite that is up in the air. The kite can be raised off the ground in the vertical position by pulling back on the right hand while maintaining the balanced position.

## SLOW MOTION REVOLUTION

This is the most challenging of all the control variation for the Revolution Kite. The objective is to hover the kite just above the ground, straight down wind, and cause it to very slowly rotate about its center. When you can do this maneuver, you will have truly mastered the control of the revolution kite. Here is what it takes:

Hover the kite in the vertical position about 5 feet above the ground with the right tip up. The leading edge will be pointing to your left, your right hand should be slightly back and your left hand should be slightly forward. I like to have my right hand higher than my left, while hovering in this vertical position. This hand position reminds me that the right tip is up at this point. As the kite rotates 180 degrees, the hand position will switch to the left hand up and back, and the right hand down and forward.

The Thumbs will alternate between pointing back when the kite is horizontal with the leading edge up, and pointing toward the kite when it is horizontal with the trailing edge up.

|       RIGHT TIP UP       |        UPRIGHT        |
| :----------------------: | :-------------------: |
|      |   |
|       LEFT TIP UP        |        INVERTED       |
|      |   |

# 3-D FLYING

3-D Flying is an unusually active method of manipulating a kite. It involves causing the kite to fly to you whereby you will catch it, and then toss it back out to the end of the short fly lines. I use 20 foot long, 80lb. test fly lines. There is more versatiliy in maneuvers when the winds are less than 5mph. Zero wind provides additional opportunities. This type of flying is also called "Catch and Throw."

Place both handles in the left hand. With the right hand, grasp the top set of fly lines about 10 inches in front of the handles.

Give a hard jerk on the top set of fly lines and the kite will come sailing toward you, leading edge first. Release the lines from your right hand and catch the kite in the center of the leading edge.

Fly the kite to the top of the wind window.  Place both handles in the left hand.  Grasp the two top fly lines about 10 inches above the handles.  Give a short jerk on the lines and the kite will come falling toward you,  leading edge first. Reach up and catch it in the center of the leading edge.

With the bridle side down, toss the kite out to the end of the fly lines.  As the right hand pushes the kite out, add a slight amount of horizontal rotation to the kite by pulling the right hand across the front of your body.  Immediately take the right handle into the right hand and  point both thumbs toward the kite.  This should stall the kite with the leading edge down as soon as it gets to the end of the fly lines.

# *18* TEAM FLYING

# BASICS

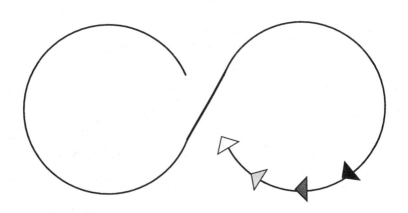

# INTRODUCTION

The thrill of team flying, for the first time, will surely inspire you to look forward to the next opportunity with anxious anticipation. This presentation provides a uniform solid foundation in the basics of team flying; when that next opportunity presents itself, you will be able to perform your part with confidence. It is exhilarating to fly synchronized maneuvers especially when there is timing required to avoid a collision. It is also exhilarating when you finish a set and the crowd behind you applauds. It doesn't take a lot of practice to have a good time team flying.

# CONSIDERATIONS

Here are just a few things you should consider to make team flying easier:

1.     The individual flyers should have good basic control of their kite. The basic skills required include smooth steering and speed control.

2.     When there are just two flyers, the more experienced person should follow.

3.     When there are more than two flyers, the more experienced flyer should lead the group. And, the least experienced flyer should be the last in line.

4.     Although it is not absolutely necessary, each flyer's length of fly line should be about 5 feet longer than that of the following kite. This will reduce the amount of bad turbulence experienced by the following kite. When a kite hits the turbulence created by another kite, the feeling is similar to hitting a speed bump, while driving your car, at about 10 miles per hour.

5.     140 feet to 150 feet is a comfortable length of fly line for the leader's kite. Small fields may require the leader's length to be 110 feet.

This presentation assumes that the leader is standing on the right side of the group. The flyers should stand about 5 to 8 feet apart. The flyers should be able to see the flyer on their right. If the lead flyer moves, then the rest of the team should move accordingly. Sometimes it may be necessary for the leader to ask the group to walk right, or left, forward, or backward.

All team flying starts with the "Follow-the-Leader" patterns of horizontal figure eights. The kites will fly up on a diagonal across the center of the wind window and down at the edges of the wind window. This specific pattern can be changed to display several different pictures.

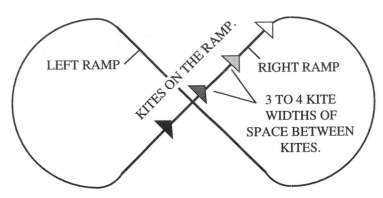

Basic Turns will be executed while the kites are on the ramps.

FLATTEN THE RAMPS OF THE FIGURE
EIGHT INTO GROUND PASSES. TURN
UP, OUT, AND DOWN TO REVERSE
THE DIRECTION OF THE GROUND PASS.
THE TURN IS CALLED A "BUTTON HOOK."

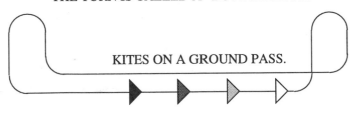

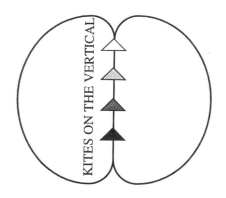

FLY THE RAMPS OF
THE FIGURE EIGHT ON
A VERTICAL PATH.

**Organized Communication** is essential for the "Execution" of synchronized team flying. The communication is accomplished by **"PREPARATORY"** and **"EXECUTION"** commands.

A **"PREPARATORY COMMAND"** is a name assigned to a sequence of maneuvers that the kites will present as a specific picture in the sky. The "Preparatory" commands should be meaningful to the pictures that are presented. This will make it easier for the flyers to remember their individual parts. In the section called "3-PERSON TEAM" I have diagramed the pictures, "Fountain" and "Boomerang."

An **"EXECUTION COMMAND"** is a word that signals the flyers to start a maneuver that is part of the picture that was called for by the preceding "Preparatory" command. These are short one-syllable words such as, "TURN," "BREAK," or "NOW." Some pictures can be presented with a single "Execution" command, while others may require as many as ten "Execution" commands.

IMPORTANT NOTE: Do not try to execute precisely on the word, "TURN." A consistent tempo is required to insure a synchronized execution. The flyers should pull on the unspoken word, *and*, in the sequence;

"TURN" *and* "BREAK" *and* "NOW" *and*.

The team leader gives a "Preparatory" command well before the kites reach the area where the "Execution" commands are to take place.   This command will alert the flyers to the sequence of maneuvers required to perform the intended pattern in the sky.  As the "Execution" commands are given by the leader, the flyers will execute their individual parts.  The end result will be a synchronized presentation of the pattern.   As the patterns are linked together, the performance becomes a routine.

## BASIC TURNS

Basic turns are defined with simple "Preparatory" commands which usually start with the direction.   The direction, "Left" or "Right," refers to the hand that you would pull to execute the turn, as opposed to the side of the sky that the kite is going to turn toward.  It should be understood that "Push Turns" are a part of any performance. However, for interpretation of the commands, the direction command should mean which hand you would "Pull" to execute the turn.  This concept allows consistent terminology regardless of the direction in which the kites are flying.

TERMINOLOGY:  The goal is to fly a routine with a minimum amount of dialogue.  Therefore, the words selected as "Preparatory" commands should be as short and to the point as possible.  It is with this thought in mind that I present the terminology that was used by my world championship team.  The terminology for the "Preparatory" and "Execution" commands of the basic team turns is presented in the following diagrams.   The words in "quotes" represent the spoken words of the leader at that approximate location in the pattern.  The interpretation of the "Preparatory" command is provided adjacent to the diagram.  The diagrams are shown with 4 kites.  However, the same terminology applies for 2 kites as well as any other number of kites.

## BASIC TURNS and their PREPARATORY COMMANDS

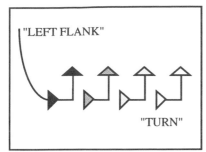

### "LEFT-FLANK"

All kites turn 90 degrees in the direction stated.

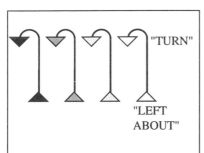

### "LEFT-ABOUT"

All kites turn 180 degrees in the direction stated.

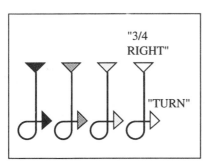

### "3/4-RIGHT"

All kites turn 270 degrees in the direction stated.

### "LEFT"

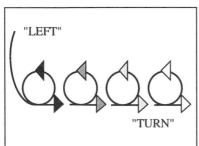

All kites turn 360 degrees in the direction stated. The size of the circle should be about 20 feet in diameter unless otherwise specified by the leader. A "TIGHT LEFT" is a wing-tip turn.

"Preparatory" command **MODIFIERS** are used to change the execution of these turns. **"ODD-EVEN," "UP,"** and **"BRACKET"** are common modifiers. The following diagrams illustrate some basic applications of these modifiers.

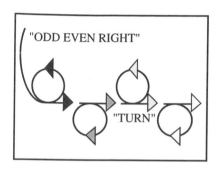

### "ODD-EVEN RIGHT"

1st and 3rd kites turn 360° to the right. 2nd and 4th kites turn 360° to the left. The modifier ODD-EVEN requires that the odd numbered kites turn the direction stated and the even numbered kites turn the opposite direction.

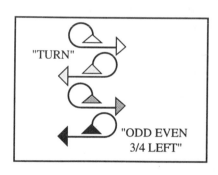

### "ODD-EVEN 3/4 LEFT"

1st and 3rd kites turn 270° to the left. 2nd and 4th kites turn 270° to the right. The net result is a Horizontal Thread. When kites pass each other in opposite directions, it is called a Thread. (Thread the Needle)

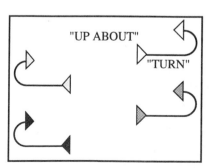

### "UP-ABOUT"

All kites turn up 180° and fly back toward the center. "DOWN-ABOUT" is another option.

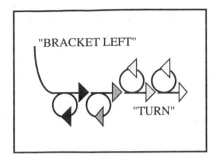

### "BRACKET-LEFT"

1st and 2nd kites turn 360° to the left.  3rd and 4th kites turn 360° to the right.  The modifier BRACKET divides the team into separate pairs. The 3rd kite is the leader of the second pair.

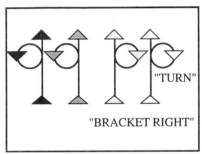

### "BRACKET-RIGHT"

1st pair of kites turns 360° to the right.  2nd pair of kites turns 360° to the left.  This turn is in the category of Mirror Image Maneuvers.

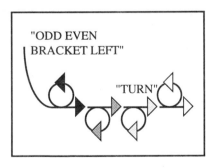

### "ODD-EVEN BRACKET-LEFT"

The leaders of the pairs turn 360° in the appropriate direction for a "Bracket-Left." The followers in each pair turn 360° in the opposite direction for the "Odd-Even."

Another modifier is the word **"FULL."**  It requires that each kite completes a FULL 360° turn in the appropriate direction before executing the basic turn.  For instance, a **"FULL-LEFT-ABOUT"** would call for the kites to make a full 360° left turn and then continue turning an additional 180° to fly back in the direction they originally came from.

So far we have looked at "Follow-the-Leader" and "Side-by-Side" formations of the team.    Another very common formation is the "Box."   Boxes can be flown in a variety of directions.   Horizontal and vertical paths can be flown in either direction. When a box is flown on a diagonal path, it becomes a diamond. Here are a few graceful methods of changing from the "Follow-the-Leader" formation to the "Box" formation.

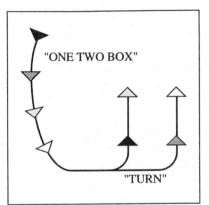

### "ONE-TWO-BOX"

1st and 2nd kites flank on the "Execution" command, "TURN."   3rd and 4th kites follow to form the "Box."

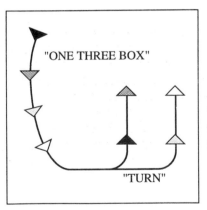

### "ONE-THREE-BOX"

1st and 3rd kites flank on the "Execution" command "TURN." 2nd and 4th kites follow to form the "Box."

The choice between these two "BOX" formations will be determined by the fly line requirements of the subsequent maneuvers.   "BOX" formations can be flown on horizontal paths if the "Execution" command is given while the kites are on a dive down the left or right side of the wind window.

These figures illustrate establishing and maintaining the Diamond formation.

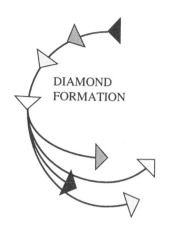

DIAMOND FORMATION

THE 2nd KITE ACCELERATES AND SWINGS WIDE. THE 3rd KITE SLOWS AND CUTS INSIDE. THE 4th KITE ACCELERATES AND FOLLOWS THE PATH OF THE LEADER.

LEADER GOES FIRST.

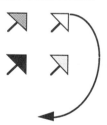

2nd AND 3rd BREAK AS SOON AS LEADER IS CLEAR OF 2nd KITE.

1 | 2

4 | 3    4th KITE BREAKS AS SOON AS 3rd KITE IS PAST.

RESUME DIAMOND FORMATION

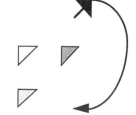

Most of the basic turns can be executed while the kites are in a "Diamond" formation. The flyers will execute their parts as though they were in a "Follow-the-Leader" formation. For instance, the "ODD-EVEN" modifier requires that the 1st and 3rd kites turn the direction stated and the 2nd and 4th kites turn the opposite direction. Therefore, the leader must consider the direction in which each kite is going to turn when using the modifiers.

LEFT TURN

ODD EVEN LEFT TURN

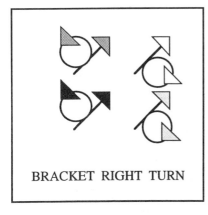

BRACKET RIGHT TURN

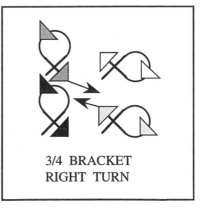

3/4 BRACKET
RIGHT TURN

It is not unusual to alter the path of the ideal basic turn in order to create a special effect. In the 3/4-Bracket-Right Turn, shown above, the 2nd and 3rd kites altered the ideal path to avoid a collision and create a Thread-the-Needle from the Diamond Formation. This maneuver is also called a Diamond-Split.

Another simple team maneuver is the "Star-Burst." From a ground pass, on the "Execution" command, all kites will make a sharp turn and fly straight toward their preassigned location in the sky. Divide the sky into equal parts and distribute the kites evenly.

These same positions are assigned to the kites for the command, "Fire-Drill." No "Execution" command is given. All kites will go to their positions and wait for further instructions. The "Fire-Drill" command can be given by any flyer who sees a potential problem or who is having a problem. Examples include: A spectator entering the flying area; or, a flyer getting sun screen in an eye.

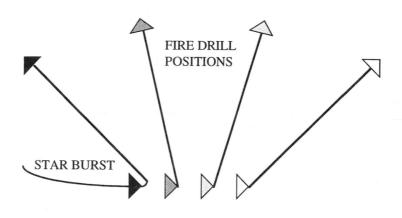

FIRE DRILL
POSITIONS

STAR BURST

## "FALL-IN"

The term, "Fall-In," is given by the leader to start the formation flying. No "Execution" command is given. All flyers turn toward the leader and take their appropriate positions in the "Follow-the-Leader" formation.

# FLY  THE  SPACE

The learning curve for team flyers has several plateaus. The first plateau is the ability to follow the kite in front of you. At this point you are focusing most of your attention on your own kite, and just trying to keep it in line. In the second plateau, you will start focusing about 80 percent of your attention on the kite in front of you and only 20 percent on your own kite. This will allow you to react more quickly to any changes in direction. At this time, you will be striving to make your kite the tail of the kite in front of you. You will also become more aware of the **SPACE** between your kite and the one in front of you. In the third plateau, you will learn to focus on the space between your kite and the one in front of you. At this point, you seldom look directly at any specific kite. All of your focus is on the space between the kites. You will be surprised at how uniform the whole team looks, when all the flyers are **FLYING THE SPACE** and all the spaces are equal. New teams should be sure to spend some time on plateaus 1 and 2 before attempting to advance to the 3rd plateau.

Maintaining a constant space, with the kites in a "Follow-the-Leader" formation, is challenging when the kites are rounding the corners of a horizontal figure eight. The leader must realize that the kites closest to the edge of the wind window have the least amount of wind. The leader's kite must slow down, so as not to run away from the kites that have not yet made the corner. The following flyers should execute a Pull Pull turn to maintain the speed of their kite as it turns the corner.

## WRAPS AND LINE TWISTS

If an individual kite makes a complete loop, the kite's fly lines will be twisted. A complete loop in the other direction will remove the twist. Most quality fly line will allow good control of the kite with 8 complete twists in the lines. I once test-flew with new 300lb. Spectra in a 6mph wind. I put 40 twists in one direction before I felt that I could no longer adequately control the kite. Leaving these twists in the line, I then sprayed the lines over the twisted area with a silicone lubricant. I added another 30 twists in the same direction before I thought that the control of the kite was unacceptable.

While in the "Follow-the-Leader" formation, if the kites complete a circle, then the fly lines of the kites will be twisted. This is called a "Wrap." A complete circle in the other direction will "Unwrap" the twist. Wraps are very common during team flying. It is very important that all fly lines are the same type and strength. I recommend at least 200 lb test for "Wraps." Some world class teams wrap with 80 lb. test. My team uses 300 lb. test when executing Compound Wraps.

## FALSE WRAP

A false wrap is created when one pair of lines slides over another pair of lines and the lines are not under very much tension. To illustrate this, lay two long pieces of string side by side across your leg. Now, slide your hand over the top of these strings and notice how they twist. When this happens to your fly lines, you will not be able to control your kite. The lines are said to be "Locked-Up." To prevent this from happening, keep your hands spread about 16 inches apart when executing a wrap, especially the Compound Wrap.

# 19 TEAM WARM-UP

## INTRODUCTION

My approach may be more rigid than most. However, I have found it to be successful in achieving the objective of the team. Namely, to be recognized as:

## "THE BEST IN THE WORLD"

There is a time for social flying, and a time for serious practice. This section is directed at the serious practice for those teams that would like to be world class. There is a certain amount of physical exertion required while flying controllable kites. Each individual has a responsibility, to the other members of the team, to be mentally and physically prepared for practice and competition. This article presents the team warm-up that takes place after the individual warm up. The leader, either alone or through a consensus of the team members, should have specific objectives in mind for the practice session.

**FALL-IN:** When the leader calls **"FALL-IN,`"** all flyers should assume their respective positions in the flight pattern. All flyers should be silent and follow the commands of the leader. The first consideration should be spacing. Remember to *fly the space.*

## WARM-UP PATTERN #1

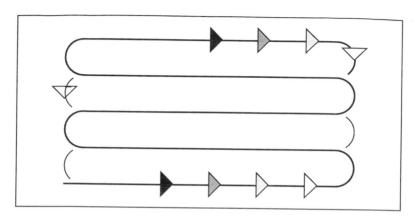

The leader should fly a series of long horizontal passes. All flyers should make sure that their kite stays an equal space from the one in front. Maintaining constant spacing at the corners is difficult. Each flyer should use a "PULL / PULL" turn on the corners. The change in elevation between the horizontal lines should be about 20 feet. The leader should determine the location of these elevations. This pattern should be maintained for at least 4 cycles. It is not necessary for the leader to make any calls during this part of the warm-up.

## ELEVATION LABLES OF THE WIND WINDOW

"FULL SKY"

"THREE QUARTER SKY"

"HALF SKY"

"QUARTER SKY"

"GROUND PASS"

The leader can describe the size of a unison turn by using the elevation lables as "Preparatory" commands. As the team is lead into a ground pass from left to right, the leader could call "FULL SKY LEFT" followed by the "Execution" command, "TURN." All kites will carve a large left circle, while continuing to maintain horizontal spacing and constant speed. The tops of the circles will be at the "FULL SKY" elevation. Similarly, turns of "HALF SKY" and "QUARTER SKY" should also be practiced. The turns should be initiated from all of the different elevations, resulting in both up and down turns. Practicing the Half Sky circles will improve the teams performance of the Team Eights Compulsory.

"ODD-EVEN, HALF-SKY, LEFT, VERTICAL, FIGURE EIGHT"

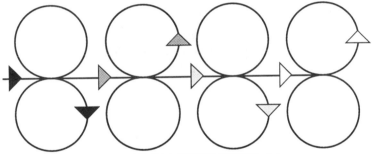

STUNT CLASSIFICATION: 1A

Here is a challenge for your team. Establish a half sky horizontal pass from left to right. When all kites are on the line, execute an "ODD-EVEN, HALF-SKY, LEFT, VERTICAL, FIGURE EIGHT." Carve the first half sky circle and meet on the "Half-Sky" line, where each will then immediately carve into the opposite half sky circle. All kites will finish at the same time, back on the "Half-Sky" line. An "Execution" command should be given to start the figure, and, then again, at the start of the second circle. For practice purposes, the leader could call, "MARK" each time the center spine of his kite is exactly vertical at the 3 and 9 o'clock positions. The other flyers will compare this to the angle of the spine on their kite, and make the necessary corrections to align with the leader.

## WARM-UP PATTERN #2

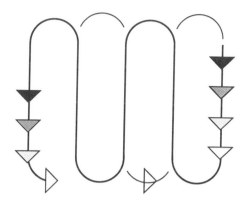

WARM-UP PATTERN #2 can be initiated by the simple command, "FOLLOW." Pattern #2 is similar to pattern #1, except that the parallel lines are vertical. The kites should be flown as high as possible and as near to the ground as possible. Particular attention should be given to flying straight vertical lines with all the kites in perfect alignment. The length of the path should allow all the kites to be on the same line at the same time. All flyers should be walking backward while the kites are going up, and walking forward while the kites are going down in order to maintain the kites at a constant speed. The kites going down must be slowed, so that they don't run away from the kites which are still going up.

I believe that a team's ability to maintain a CONSTANT SPEED throughout a maneuver is PARAMOUNT in the performance of compulsory figures.


"CONSTANT TENSION EQUALS CONSTANT SPEED"

## WARM-UP TURN PATTERNS

No warm-up period would be complete without unison turns in both directions. During the execution of these turns, all members should make every effort to give the appearance that the kites are attached like the wheels on a train.

## WARM-UP CLOSE ORDER DRILL

The next warm-up exercise is to REDUCE THE SPACING. Fly as tight a spacing as you can possibly get away with. A world class objective for spacing is to fly with less than one kite's width between the kites. However, you must not fly so closely that the nose of the following kite is touching the fly lines of the kite in front. When flying unison turns, during the close order drill, the wing tips should overlap. Now start over with WARM-UP PATTERN #1 and work your way through all of the patterns, again.

### WARM-UP WRAPS

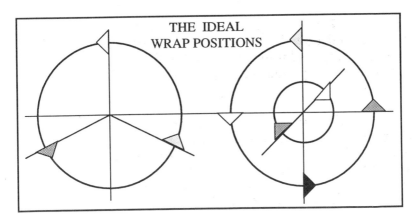

THE IDEAL
WRAP POSITIONS

Wraps are the final warm-up exercise. Practice establishing and maintaining the Ideal Wrap Positions in both the clockwise and counterclockwise directions.

# HAZARDS TO YOUR KITE & STRINGS

* **Extremely Hot Weather:**   Most kites have plastic parts that will become soft in hot weather. They may change shape and affect the way your kite flies.. If the kite strings lie on the hot pavement of a parking lot, you may have problems. The wax on Kevlar will make the line stiff. The heat sensitivity of Spectra may result in deterioration.

* **Extremely Cold Weather:**   Some of the sticks used in kites become brittle and break more easily in extremely cold weather. You should check with the dealer to see if your kite requires any concern for cold weather.

* **Fences:**   Chained Link and Barbed Wire fences have torn many kites; they seem to like it. The droop in the wire between the posts resembles a smile--I Think.

* **Trees, Bushes, Cactus, etc.**   Flying your kite over and around  trees, bushes, and cactus can be fun, but do not be surprised if they reach out and grab your kite. I like to land in tree tops and paste onto light poles, but I do it with great caution.

* **Salt Water**:  The salt in sea water can corrode the aluminum parts used to join the sticks together. If you dip your kite into sea water be sure to separate the joints of the kite and wash them thoroughly with fresh water. Leave them apart to dry.  Playing with the kite on the water can be challenging and provide a lot of enjoyment.

# 20 BUILDING

# A

# ROUTINE

Building a routine is easiest if you apply a systematic process. The process will involve decisions based on the objectives of the routine. Extemporaneous and Recreational routines are quite different from the ones that are designed to impress judges. This presentation is general and is intended to show you the basic systematic process. This block diagram shows the path of the decision-making process.

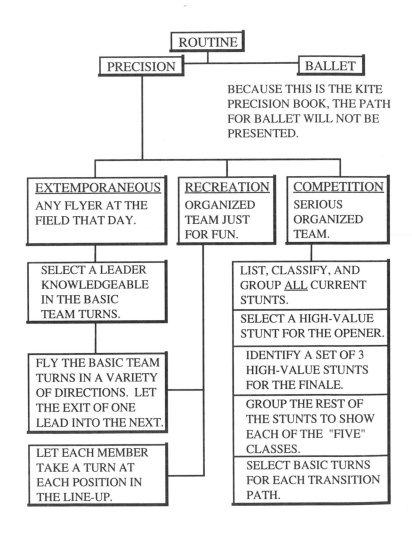

## EXTEMPORANEOUS

Any flyer can enjoy the excitement of team flying. Any flyer with a knowledge of the basic team turns can lead a team of novice flyers. Use the following list for starters:

1. Establish a horizontal figure eight pattern.
2. Identify the "Fire Drill" positions for each flyer.
3. While the fliers are hovering in their "Fire Drill" positions, demonstrate a 360° left turn in the size you want them to fly. Stress that the words, "LEFT" and "RIGHT," refer to the hand with which they will pull, as opposed to the side of the sky the kite will fly toward.
4. Give a description of "Preparatory" commands and "Execution" commands.
5. Lead the group through several figure eights. Call for the "LEFT" and "RIGHT" turns while the kites are on the ramps.
6. Call for a "Fire Drill." Describe the concept of the "ODD-EVEN" modifier. Identify which flyers in the group will turn in the direction stated and which flyers will turn in the opposite direction.
7. Lead the group through several figure eights. Call for the "ODD-EVEN LEFT" and "ODD-EVEN RIGHT" turns while the kites are on the ramps.
8. Let the flyers know when you are going to mix regular turns with odd-even turns.
9. Call for a "Fire Drill." Demonstrate a "LEFT-FLANK" from a ground pass and a "RIGHT-ABOUT" at the top of the wind window, and then another "LEFT-FLANK" at the bottom.
10. Lead the group through several sequences of the "LEFT-FLANK," "RIGHT-ABOUT," and "LEFT-FLANK."
11. Let the flyers know you are going to call turns on the vertical paths.
12. Call for a "RIGHT TURN" while the kites are going up and a "LEFT TURN" while the kites are coming down.

13. Assign a "Preparatory" command name to the mini routine "left-flank, right-turn, right-about, left-turn, left flank." After you give the "Preparatory" command, you will only need to call the "Execution" commands to complete the mini-routine.

14. Continue this step-by-step process through all of the basic team turns.

Here are some suggested sequences that can be flown by any number of flyers. The Bracket turn for 2 people is the same as an Odd-Even turn. The Bracket turn for 3 people allows the center person to choose which flyer to pair with. Once the choice is made, it must be consistent throughout the sequence. However, it may be changed in a subsequent sequence.

From a left to right ground pass, execute the sequence of turns in a group, one right after the other.

| "3/4 SERIES" | "BRACKETS" | "STAIRS" |
|---|---|---|
| left flank | left flank | left flank (at edge) |
| 3/4 right | bracket right | left flank |
| 3/4 left | right about | right flank |
| right flank | bracket left | left flank |
| 3/4 left | left flank | right flank |
| 3/4 right | | right flank |

From a Follow-The-Leader up the center, execute the sequence of turns in a group, one right after the other.

| "SERIES 8's" | "CENTER SPLIT" | "SQUARES" |
|---|---|---|
| bracket right | odd-even 3/4 left | 3 right flanks |
| odd-even right | up about | pass thru |
| odd-even left | pass thru | 2 right flanks |
| bracket left | up about | pass thru |
| large odd-even left | pass thru | 2 left flanks |
| large odd-even right | odd-even 3/4 right | right flank in mid. |

## RECREATION

All teams should set aside some time for recreational flying. This provides an opportunity for the team to experiment with new ideas. Each member of the team should take a turn flying the lead position as well as the other positions in the line-up. This will provide each of the team members with a better understanding of the problems that exist within a specific pattern. Flying the sequences presented in the Extemporaneous section, will be a review of the fundamentals and reinforce the teams foundation. Link as many of the basic team turns together as you can and assign the sequence a "Preparatory" command.

## COMPETITION

The teams interested in serious competition, will need to develop stunts in each of the 5 fundamental classes. As their experience grows, they will need to expand their collection of stunts to include each of the degrees of difficulty correlating with each of the fundamental classes. I suggest that the team establish a stunt log-book, because, as the team's collection of stunts expands, it is easy to forget some earlier useful stunts.

The opening stunt should capture the attention of the judges. It should say "We Have Arrived!!" Each element should be performed with such smoothness and precise kite positioning that the thoughts of the judges and spectators alike would include words such as "WOW," "OH MY," and "THAT WAS INCREDIBLE." In the middle of the routine, there should be a couple of surprises in which the set-up may look like a very common stunt. Then, at the last moment, something unexpected happens! The stall maneuvers are good surprise elements.

When you create a new involved maneuver that places the fly lines into a peculiar twist or wrap, be just as creative with the design of a clearing maneuver. Don't just reverse the pattern to clear the lines.

When one of your flyers has developed a specific skill, try to design a stunt that will feature that special skill. Place these stunts near the middle of the routine.

If your routine requires an extended Follow-The-Leader path, then be sure to insert one of the basic team turns on that path. The transitions between major elements of a routine are a definite consideration in the scoring.

The routine should utilize the entire wind window. Include some Edge-Work. However, be aware of the field boundaries when executing Edge-Work. If any part of any one of the kites goes over the boundary, your team could be disqualified. In the routine your right side edge work should be well separated from your left side edge work so that you have time to reposition your bodies on the field. The routine should include some elements near the ground and on the ground, unless there are specific rules against it.

## BE SURE YOU KNOW THE RULES!!!

Some contests may have slight variations from the standard rules. Consider your routine relative to the rules. If your routine has any stunts that could be misinterpreted as a kite out of control or a mid-air collision, be sure to advise the judges via the field director. For instance, tell the field director to notify the judges that in the opening sequence of the routine, two of the kites will collide in mid-air locking their noses together for a short period of time. If the judges have not been notified ahead of time about this type of action, the routine would surely suffer a deduction for a mid-air collision.

YOUR PRECISION ROUTINE SHOULD BE DESIGNED TO DEMONSTRATE YOUR TEAM'S ABILITY TO FLY PRECISE SYNCHRONIZED PATTERNS.

# *21* CLASSES

## and

## DEGREE of
## DIFFICULTY

## for

# TEAM STUNTS

There are 5 fundamental classes of team stunts:

Class 1. Follow-the-Leader and Side-by-Side
Class 2. Mirror-Image
Class 3. Displacement
Class 4. Stall
Class 5. Contact

1.  Unison turns in the Follow-the-Leader and Side-by-Side formations form the most fundamental class of stunts.

2.  Mirror-Image patterns form the second class of stunts.  At the same time, and on the left side of the wind widow, the 3rd and 4th kites will execute a mirror image of the patterns that the 1st and 2nd kites are executing on the right side of the wind window.

3.  Displacement patterns form the third class of stunts.  One, or more, of the kites will leave the group in order to create a special effect, and then rejoin the group later in the pattern.  The "Water Fountain" and the "Boomerang," diagramed in the 3-PERSON TEAM section of the book, fit into this class of stunts.

4.  Stall patterns form the fourth class of stunts.  Very interesting pictures can be created by stalling one or more of the kites, momentarily, in the middle of the sky.  It is quite popular to have one or more kites fly completely around a stalled kite.

5.  Contact stunts form the fifth class.  Contact stunts involve one kite's intentional contact with another kite or its fly lines.  A kite's intentional contact with the ground is also included in this category.  Refueling is a contact stunt, whereby the following kite moves so closely behind another kite that its nose is wedged between the fly lines of that kite.  When a kite is flown so closely to the ground that one of its tips is intentionally dragged across the ground, the stunt is called a Tip-Drag.

The degree of difficulty for team stunts is separated into 5 categories:

> Type A. General
> Type B. Timing 1
> Type C. Timing 2
> Type D. Speed Control
> Type E. Fly Line

Type A. <u>All kites are flying in their own space.</u> No other kites are crossing their path. Follow-the-Leader figure eights with Unison Turns, as well as Horizontal and Vertical Thread-the-Needles, are stunts in this category.

Type B. <u>Timing is required to avoid a collision.</u> Stunts like the Diagonal Thread and the T-Bone are in this category.

Type C. <u>Timing is required to avoid a collision while one or more of the the kites is changing directions.</u> The Weave and the Stall-Fly-Around are in this category.

Type D. <u>Each kite needs to fly at a different speed to maintain the picture.</u> The Arrowhead maneuver and the Full-Sky Pinwheel maneuver are stunts in this category.

Type E. <u>The fly lines are intentionally twisted during flight.</u> Very complex inner twisting of the fly lines, can produce an interesting spider web picture in the sky. The Compound Wrap and the Sequential Fly-Around are stunts in this category. This is the line-breaker category. Few fly lines survive the learning process.

The classification of a team stunt is identified by the assigning of a number from the class category and a letter from the degree of difficulty category. This classification helps you to group similar stunts into a category. 1A stunts are used to introduce new fliers to the concept of team flying. World Class Teams load their routines with stunts combining Classes 3,4,& 5 with Types C,D,& E.

*"It's quite a sight to behold."*

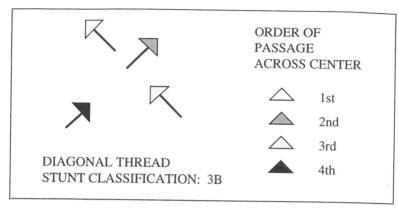

ORDER OF
PASSAGE
ACROSS CENTER

1st

2nd

3rd

4th

DIAGONAL THREAD
STUNT CLASSIFICATION: 3B

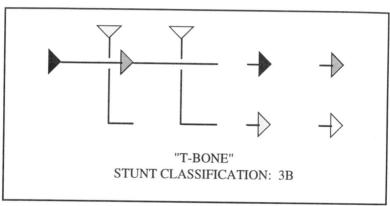

"T-BONE"
STUNT CLASSIFICATION: 3B

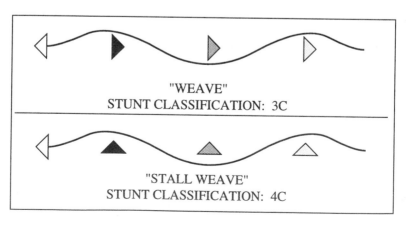

"WEAVE"
STUNT CLASSIFICATION: 3C

"STALL WEAVE"
STUNT CLASSIFICATION: 4C

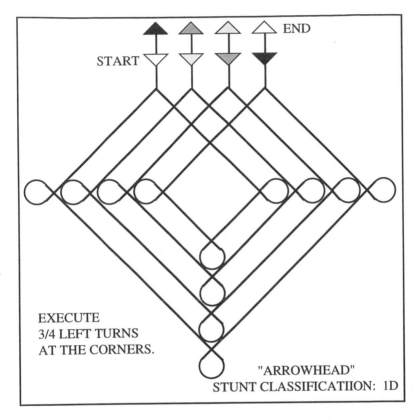

START

END

EXECUTE
3/4 LEFT TURNS
AT THE CORNERS.

"ARROWHEAD"
STUNT CLASSIFICATIION: 1D

This figure requires extensive speed control. The kite on the inside track should be on the longest fly lines. The kite on the outside track should be on the shortest fly lines. When my team flew this maneuver, the kite on the inside track was on 150ft. lines and the kite on the outside track was on 125ft. lines. At the start of the figure, the fly lines of the kite on the inside track were over the top of the other fly lines, and the fly lines of the kite on the outside track were beneath the other lines. The flyer of the kite on the inside track stood behind the other flyers at the start, and then moved forward to slow down the kite during the execution of the figure. The flyer of the kite on the outside track stood forward of the rest of the flyers at the start, and then moved backward to speed up the kite during the execution of the figure. The other two flyers balanced their movements in between.

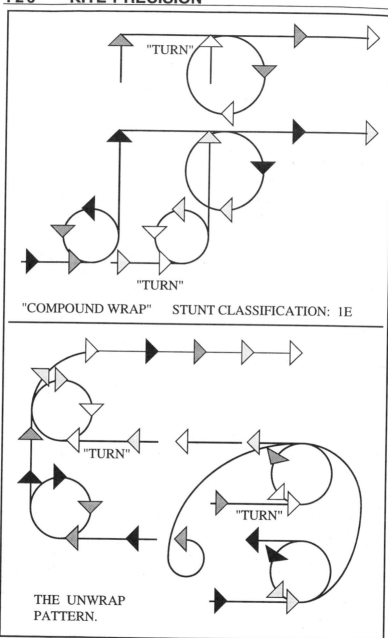

"TURN"

"TURN"

"COMPOUND WRAP"     STUNT CLASSIFICATION: 1E

"TURN"

"TURN"

THE UNWRAP
PATTERN.

*"Good Luck"*

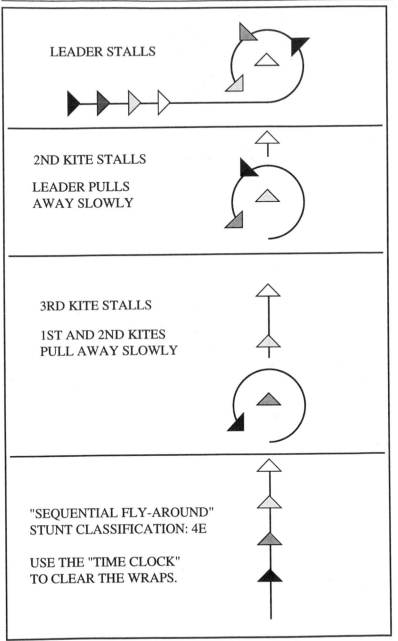

LEADER STALLS

2ND KITE STALLS

LEADER PULLS
AWAY SLOWLY

3RD KITE STALLS

1ST AND 2ND KITES
PULL AWAY SLOWLY

"SEQUENTIAL FLY-AROUND"
STUNT CLASSIFICATION: 4E

USE THE "TIME CLOCK"
TO CLEAR THE WRAPS.

*"Looks easy, doesn't it?"*

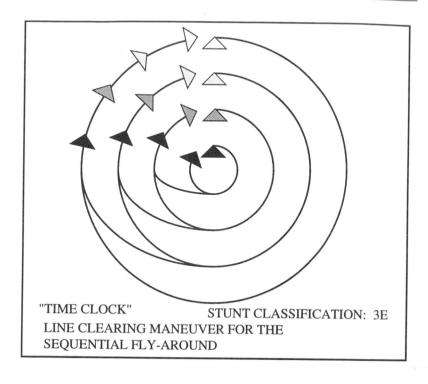

"TIME CLOCK"                    STUNT CLASSIFICATION: 3E
LINE CLEARING MANEUVER FOR THE
SEQUENTIAL FLY-AROUND

The "Sequential Fly-Around" and the "Time-Clock," are good examples of using a different stunt to clear the fly lines instead of reversing the original stunt. This is one of the most challenging aspects of team stunt design. Another challenge is the choreography of stunts. Every effort should be made to have the exit of one stunt be the entrance to the next stunt.

*I hope you enjoyed this presentation of team flying and that you will have an opportunity to experience it as I have.*

# 22 COUPLES

Two people can have a lot of fun sharing the control of one kite. Only one of the persons needs to know how to fly the kite, *"as long as the other person is willing to follow instructions,"* I said with a grin.

When I presented this concept to couples in the United States, England, France, Germany, and Japan, it was so well received that I wanted to share it with the readers of this book.

This is the basic position for two people to share the controls of one kite. The control will be easiest if one handle is held solid while the other person does all of the steering. To hold a handle solid, lock the elbow of that arm against your side. The steering handle is positioned relative to the solid handle. Take turns at both holding solid and steering.

When you are ready for the next position, maneuver the kite to the edge of the wind window, and about 50 feet above the ground. The reduced pull will allow you to pass your handle to your partner's hand. Do not let go of the handle until your partner has it.

Bring the free hands forward and assume the dance position. Hold your handle firmly against your partners body. Steer the kite by rotating your bodies together as though you were dancing. Rotate your bodies to the right for a right turn and to the left for a left turn. Caution, be careful not to let your arms interfere with the fly lines when the kite goes to the top of the wind window.

When you are ready to leave the dance position, fly the kite to the top of the wind window, and raise the hand holding the handle over your head. Take note of whose arm is in front. That person will pivot across in front of the other person for the next position.

The "Stroll In The Park" position is easiest if one handle is held solid while the other person does all the steering. Add style by extending the reach of the hand hold. You could also swing the hand hold as though you were Strolling In The Park.

Raise the hand hold and allow her to take a position in front of you. Pass your handle to her, and create the "Cuddle" position. This is a very good position when the wind is above 15 mph.

Showcase the best looking flyer for the finale.

# *23* HOW TO TIE

# BRIDLE LINES

# AND

# TRAIN LINES

This is a presentation of the most common method of tying bridle lines and train lines to equal length.

## MATERIALS REQUIRED

1. A piece of wood about 6 inches longer than the finished length of the lines you want to tie. 1 x 3 Pine works just fine. If you want to get fancy you may even want to seal it and paint it. You will be making reference marks on it.

2. Two one-inch-long finishing nails and a hammer.

3. Supply of bridle line to suit your needs. 100lb. to 150lb. Dacron is fine for most applications.

4. Felt-tipped marker. Fine or medium point is best.

5. Measuring tape.

## CONSTRUCTION

1. Pound the nails into the board 3/4 of an inch farther apart than the finished length you intend to tie. Leave 1/2 inch of the nail standing out of the board. The nails should be straight up perpendicular to the board.

2. With the felt-tipped marker, put a mark about 6 inches in from each nail on the imaginary line between the two nails.

## PROCEDURE

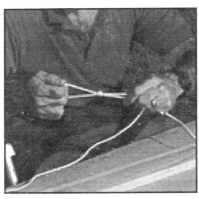

1. Fold 8 inches of the line back onto itself around one of the nails. Pinch the two sides of the loop together at the 6-inch mark from the nail. Lift the loop off the nail and tie an overhand knot in the loop to make a closed loop. The knot needs to be tightened at the pinch point to insure that all of the loops will be of equal size. This will be important when tying train line loops that need to be exactly the same length. The finished length of your loop will be shorter than 6 inches, because of the length used up in making the knot.

Note:  There is no need to cut a length from your spool of line.  Just reel off enough to work with.

2.  Place the closed loop over one of the nails on the board.  I am right handed so I place the loop over the nail on the left.

3.  Grasp the line beyond the other nail and tightly bend it around this nail to form another loop.

IMPORTANT NOTE:  To insure equal length lines, the tightness with which you pull the line around the nail should be repeated as closely as possible on subsequent loops you tie.

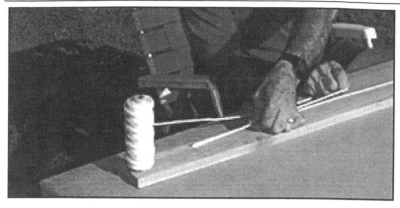

4. If you pulled the line around the nail with your right hand, then, while keeping tension on the line, pinch the pair of lines at the mark with your left thumb and forefinger. Try not to let the lines slip relative to each other as you proceed. Carefully lift the loop off of the nail with your right hand. I like to use the fingernail of my index finger to work the loop to the top of the nail. The small head of the finishing nail becomes important at this point. You can see that if the nail has a large head, it would be more difficult to remove the loop without the lines slipping.

5. Tie an overhand knot as close to the pinch point as possible to form a loop. That's the 1st bridle line of your set. Now, proceed with making more lines of the same length.

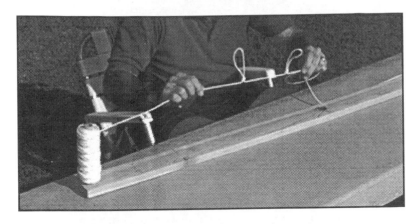

6.  Tie another loop, of the same size, a few inches away from the last loop. Pull the overhand knot tightly.

7.  Place this new loop over the nail on the left and you are ready to tie another line to match the first. Repeat from step 3.

8. When you are all finished, you will have a long line of double loops.  Carefully cut the lines apart at the short length between the loops.

And, "Voila!" There you have it!  A whole bunch of identical lengths of line with loops at both ends.

If you used Dacron, or some other similar line, you may want to heat the cut ends to seal them and keep them from fraying.

Note:   Let the nail at one end of the board be the common nail, and then add nails to the other end for additional lengths you need to tie.  Stagger these additional nails to keep them out of your way.  The added nail, closest to the common nail, should be the furthest from you.  Label each of the nails; so, you can quickly identify which bridle length you will tie with that nail.

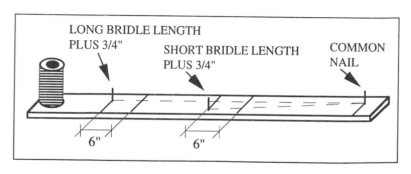

LONG BRIDLE LENGTH
PLUS 3/4"
SHORT BRIDLE LENGTH
PLUS 3/4"
COMMON NAIL
6"
6"

# *24* SETTING UP NEW LINES

Most of the lines used for flying controllable kites are *hollow braided* Spectra or Kevlar. After the braiding process, the weave is still loose. Before the lines are tied to length, it is advisable to put a considerable amount of tension on the lines to tighten the braid.

Some new lines come pre-sleeved, tied to length, and pre-stretched. Most new line is available pre-sleeved and wound onto spools in approximate lengths; no pre-stetching has been done. This section will tell you how to set up lines that are pre-sleeved, but not yet stretched or tied to length.

The sleeving on the line is about 10 inches long. Make sure that you can see some of the fly line extending from the end of the sleeving. Tie a simple overhand knot at the very end of the sleeving, so that the line will be locked inside the sleeving.

Hold the knotted end with one hand. With the other hand, pinch the sleeving between the thumb nail and forefinger. Slide this pinch down the sleeving to remove the slack from the sleeving. I call this "milking the sleeving down the line."

Fold the sleeved end in half. Pinch the bend to crease it.

Tie a simple overhand knot. Make the loop as large as possible. Tighten the knot as solidly as possible. Do the same to the other line.

Slip the loops over a ground stake. I use a 3/16 diameter metal rod with a golf ball attached to one end. Place the spools onto a spare kite stick. The top spreader of a delta kite will do just fine.

Walk the lines out to the end. It is best to let the lines unroll from the spools rather than coil off the end. Coiling off the end will induce twists down the entire length of the line.

Put about 10 turns back onto the spools. This will provide a good handle for the stretching. Stay low to the ground and pull hard on the lines. Maintain a constant tension for about one minute. 150ft lines could stretch as much as 5 to 6 feet.

Put equal tension on both lines. Hold them side by side.

Use a felt tipped marker to mark the lines.

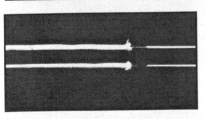

Remove the spools and slide the end of the sleeving up to the mark. Pinch the sleeving at the mark and milk it toward the handle end of the line. Fold it in half, pinch it and tie an overhand knot.

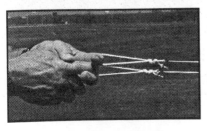

Test for equal length. When the lines are equal, tie a second knot and check again. The final line length adjustment will be done after the lines have been flown for about one hour.

# KNOTS

The two most common knots used in kiting are the Overhand and the Larks-Head.

Overhand Knot:
To form a loop in the end of a line.
To make a utility loop.

Larks-Head Knot:
To attach a utility loop to the frame.
To attach a train line to the utility loop.
To attach a bridle line to the frame.

Most flying problems experienced with a kite can be traced to at least one of 4 different causes. A General Cause and Effect Section follows the Specific Symptoms Section. Locate the symptom that best describes your problem and then turn to that section and get the necessary help.

## SPECIFIC SYMPTOMS

**Section #**

**1.0 ASSEMBLY**
1.1 Parts do not fit together.
1.2 Parts do not stay in place.
1.3 Sticks are poked through the nose.

**2.0 SETTING UP BEFORE LAUNCH**
2.1 Wind blows the kite around on the ground.
2.2 Lines become twisted or tangled.
2.3 Kite self-launches before you get to the handles.

**3.0 LAUNCHING**
3.1 Kite does not lift off the ground.
3.2 Kite turns immediately into the ground.
3.3 Kite lifts only a little in spite of a hard pull.

**4.0 FLYING**
4.1 Kite launches OK but falls out of sky at start of turn.
4.2 Kite flies OK in the center but falls out at the edge.
4.3 Kite has very little pull.
4.4 Kite has too much pull.
4.5 Kite does not climb straight overhead.

**5.0 TURNING**
5.1 Turns too big.
5.2 Turns too small.
5.3 Kite over steers the turns.
5.4 Kite collapses and falls out of the sky during turns.
5.5 Left & Right turns are different size for the same pull.

**6.0 LANDING**
6.1 Kite wants to fly instead of land.

## 1.0    ASSEMBLY

1.1    Parts do not fit together.
       If you have more than one kite, could it be that you might have gotten the parts mixed up? Not all kites have the same size spars and fittings. If this is a new kite, then contact the manufacturer or retailer to see if you have the correct parts.

1.2    Parts do not stay in place.
       If the kite is new, then contact the manufacturer or the retailer.
       If your problem is with a used kite, then the parts may be worn. Sometimes, the vinyl connectors stretch and no longer hold the spar securely. If this happens, wrap a piece of plastic electrical tape around the end of the spar before you push it into the vinyl connector. This should tighten the joint. Otherwise, wrap tape around the outside of the joint. Some kites use elastic cords hooked into arrow nocks at the tips, to hold the sail in place. If these cords are loose, then the joint at the spar may separate. Too much tension on these cords may push the spar through the sail at the other end.

1.3    Sticks are poked through the nose.
       This is caused by one of two reasons. Nose first crashes are the most common cause. The other reason is that the elastic cords that put tension on the sail are too tight. I have used Crazy Glue as a quick fix to seal the nose webbing on my kites. To prevent this from happening, wrap tape around the top end of each spar before you put it into the kite. This should cushion the sharp edges of the spar.

## 2.0    SETTING UP BEFORE LAUNCH

2.1    Wind blows the kite around on the ground.
       Always lay the kite, "bridle-face-down," with the "nose pointing into the wind." Whenever you are assembling or disassembling your kite, keep your back to the wind and the nose of the kite into the wind.

2.2    Lines become twisted or tangled.

There are many types of line winders. Some winders are turned to reel line on and off. These winders usually do not have problems, unless the line is too loose on the spool. Other winders are held stationary while the line is wound around them. A figure eight winder does not have problems unless you wind the lines too loosely. Most problems occur with the type of winder that is held stationary while you wind the lines around it. I suggest that you mark the ends of your winder with the letters "A" and "B." Now, If you hold end "A" of the winder in your left hand and wind the line around end "B" with your right hand, then it is ultra important to hold end "A" and allow the line to come off of end "B" when you remove the lines from the winder. Otherwise, by the time you get to the end, you will have hundreds of twists in the pair of lines. If this does happen, don't try to remove the twists one-by-one. Instead, examine the twists and wind the twisted set of lines back onto the winder in a direction that will remove a twist with each wrap. Then, when all the line is back on the winder, turn it around and remove the lines from the other end. Check to make sure that the twists are being removed as you start.

I wind my lines onto my handles, rather than to use a winder. I pull the handle bridle lines to one end of the handles and hold that end in my left hand. I then use my right hand to wind the lines around the handles. When I am setting up to fly, I first attach the lines to the kite. Then, I examine the handles to see which end has the bridle lines sticking out from under the fly lines. I hold that end of the handles in my left hand. I then place my right arm between the lines going to the kite. I use my right hand to help guide the lines as they are coming off of the handles. With my arm between the lines, if any twists start to develop, I will notice it right away. When I get to the end of the lines, I am ready to launch the kite.

2.3     Kite self-launches before you get to the handles.
         If you do not lean the kite back far enough, it
will self-launch. When you look at the kite from the side, you
should notice it forms two angles with the ground. The frame
makes one angle, and the back of the sail makes the second.
The driving force of the wind, is acting on the angle formed
by the back of the sail. Therefore, it is necessary for this
angle to be back far enough to force the wind to spill over the
nose of the kite, instead of under the trailing edge.

## 3.0  LAUNCHING

3.1     Kite does not lift off the ground.
         The wind does not spill off the trailing edge of
the kite. The bridle of the kite must be adjusted to bring the
nose forward. Move the bridle tow points toward the nose in
1/4 inch increments. Be sure to set both sides equal. Fine
tuning is accomplished with 1/8 inch changes.

3.2     Kite turns immediately into the ground.
         The most common reason for this is that the
flyer has accidentally held the handles in the wrong hands. If
during the launch, the kite starts to turn to the right, and you
pull on the left hand which is holding the right handle, the kite
will turn faster to the right and probably hit the ground.

*I have practiced flying my kite with the handles in opposite
hands. Sometimes, I will put a couple of twists in the lines and
then pass the handles to another flyer asking, "check out my
kite; it doesn't seem to be flying right." They usually don't
think it is as funny as I do. However, I only do this with my
kite, so that if they crash, its my kite that crashes, not theirs.*

A less common reason for the quick return to the ground is
when one of the lines is significantly shorter than the other,
or, the line is not bridled to the kite properly. First, check the
kite, and then if everything is OK, proceed with checking the
length of the fly lines. Stake the kite end of the lines to the
ground and then pull on the handle ends to see if they are
equal.

3.3    Kite lifts only a little in spite of a hard pull.
            The bridle is set too low. Move the bridle tow point toward the nose in 1/4 inch increments. Test fly each new setting until you get the proper performance. Both sides must always be equal length. Fine tuning is accomplished with 1/8 inch changes.

## 4.0    FLYING

4.1    Kite launches OK but falls out of sky at start of turn.
            The bridle is set too high. Move the bridle tow point away from the nose in 1/4 inch increments. Test fly each new setting until you get the proper performance. Be sure to set both sides equal. Fine tuning is accomplished with 1/8 inch changes.

4.2    Kite flies OK in the center but falls out at the edges.
            Two possibilities exist. The most common is that the bridle is set too high. Move the bridle tow point away from the nose in 1/8 inch increments. Test fly each new setting until you get the proper performance. The other possibility is that the sail is too flat. There is not enough billow to maintain lift at the edges. The bridle settings of kites with flat sails are more critical. Either carefully adjust the bridle or shorten the spreaders to add more billow to the sail.

4.3    Kite has very little pull.
            If the kite flies well, then it could be a characteristic of the design. If you want to add more pull, lower the bridle tow point in 1/8 inch increments. Be sure to mark the original tow point setting, so if the adjustment produces adverse performance, you can return to the original setting.

4.4    Kite has too much pull.
            If the kite flies well in lesser wind conditions, then the amount of pull could be a characteristic of the design. If you want to reduce the amount of pull, raise the bridle tow point in 1/8 inch increments. Be sure to mark the original tow point setting, so if the adjustment produces adverse performance, you can return to the original setting.

4.5    Kite does not climb straight overhead.
The most common reason for this is that the bridle tow points are set too low. Move the bridle tow points toward the nose in 1/8 inch increments. Test fly each setting with turns at the edge of the wind window, to make sure that you have not created a new problem. Another possibility is too much drag on too long and/or too heavy a weight of fly line. 200 feet of 500lb. line will keep a 6 foot delta from climbing straight overhead.

## 5.0    TURNING

5.1    Turns too big.
The bridle is set too high. Move the bridle tow points away from the nose in 1/8 inch increments. Test each new setting until you get the kite to execute a turn with a diameter that is about twice the width of the kite.

5.2    Turns too small.
The bridle is set too low. Move the bridle tow points toward the nose in 1/8 inch increments. Test each new setting until you get the kite to execute a turn with a diameter that is about twice the width of the kite.

5.3    Kite over-steers the turns.
Some brands of kites are designed to fly with that characteristic. Check with the manufacturer or the dealer. If it is not a designed performance characteristic, then the bridle tow points are set too low. Move the bridle tow points toward the nose in 1/8 inch increments. Some over-steering can be eliminated by using the "PULL-PULL" technique to execute the turns. Always maintain tension in both lines.

5.4    Kite collapses and falls out of the sky during turns.
Two possibilities exist. The most common is that the bridle is set too high. Move the bridle tow points away from the nose in 1/4 inch increments. Test fly each new setting. Fine tuning is done with 1/8 inch adjustments. The other possibility is that the sail is too flat. There is not enough billow in the sail to maintain lift during the turn. Shorten the spreader bars to add more billow. Caution--balance problems may be created with this solution.

5.5    Left & Right turns are different size for the same pull.
One reason could be that the fly lines are not equal length. Use the straight line flight method to check for equal length fly lines. Another reason could be that the connector between the bottom spreaders and the center spine has shifted, creating more billow on one side and reducing billow on the other. Examine the connector and make the proper adjustment if necessary. All testing for equal sized right and left turns should be conducted straight down wind and at the same elevation. Otherwise, the turns will be different because of the influences of the wind.

## 6.0   LANDING

6.1    Kite wants to fly instead of land.
The bridle is set too high. Move the bridle tow points away from the nose in 1/8 inch increments. There are several landing techniques. All of them require removing the wind pressure from the sail. Using the "PUSH-PUSH" turn is the most effective way of removing the wind pressure from the sail of the kite.

## GENERAL CAUSE AND EFFECT

### THE BRIDLE TOW POINTS ARE SET TOO <u>CLOSE</u> TO THE NOSE.

When the nose of the kite is tilted forward, then more wind will spill-off the trailing edge of the kite.

When too much wind is allowed to spill-off the trailing edge, the kite will have very little pull.

Near the ground the kite will want to fly, making it very difficult to land.

High in the sky and on the edge, the wind goes over the nose and deflates the sail, causing the kite to collapse and fall to the ground.

When executing a turn, the sail surface which is supposed to catch the wind, is spilling so much wind that the turning force is very small and the kite makes a much larger turn.

When executing a turn, if you pull too much the wind will push on the back side of the kite, collapsing the sail, and the kite will fall out of the sky.

### REMEDY:

Make the top leg of the bridle longer by moving the tow point down away from the nose. Make 1/8 to 1/4 inch adjustments and then test fly. The bridles on both sides of the kite must be equal. Use the leading edges, center spine, and bottom spreaders, as references, to compare the settings of the right and left side bridles.

## THE BRIDLE TOW POINTS ARE SET TOO <u>FAR</u> FROM THE NOSE.

When the nose of the kite is tilted too far back, more wind will spill over the nose and the leading edges.

In an extreme case, the kite will not come off the ground, no matter how hard you pull.

In a less extreme case, the kite will lift off the ground a few feet, however, it will be difficult to fly.

The kite will make very tight turns.

When the nose of the kite is just a little too far back, the kite will pull hard.

The kite will not climb to a point straight up overhead.

## <u>REMEDY:</u>

Make the top leg of the bridle shorter, by moving the tow point toward the nose. The bridles on both sides of the kite must be equal. Use the leading edge, center spine, and bottom spreaders, as references, to compare the settings of the right and left side bridles.

## ONE OF THE LINES IS LONGER THAN THE OTHER.

In the extreme case, the kite will turn immediately into the ground when you try to launch.

The kite makes different sized turns to the left and right even though you are pulling the same for both directions.

The kite always wants to turn in the same direction while you are holding your hands even.

## 3 CAUSES FOR UNEQUAL LINES:

One of the fly lines and/or a bridle line is twisted around one of the sticks.

If your lines are new, they may have stretched.

If your lines are old, there could be many more twists in one of the lines than in the other. Look down the length of the line in the direction of the sun--NOT DIRECTLY INTO THE SUN--but in that general direction. Try it. I think you will be surprised at how the twists show up from that angle.

## REMEDY:

Correct any fly line or bridle line assembly problems at the kite.

Stretch new lines. See the section of the book about Setting Up New Lines.

If a line has developed an excessive amount of twists, stake the kite end of the line to the ground and dangle the handle end about a foot below your hand. Put a small amount of tension in the line while you spin the handle in the appropriate direction to remove the twists.

Here is another method for removing twists from a single line. Stake the handle end firmly to the ground. Then, starting at the handle, pinch the line tightly between two pieces of wooden dowel. Maintain a tight pinch and walk toward the other end of the line while you let the line slide through the dowels. I call this "milking the twists out of the line." An interesting phenomenon takes place that had puzzled me for some time. The line that had just been "milked," got shorter, even though a lot of twists had been removed. My conclusion was that the pinching process had loosened the weave in the line. Therefore, lines need to be stretched after milking.

## THE FRAME OF THE KITE IS DISTORTED

When the frame of the kite is distorted, the flight characteristics are not the same for turns in both directions. If the center spine connector, which most delta kites have, shifts by as little as 1/4 of an inch, the right and left turns will be different sizes. The shift changes the effective length of the bottom spreaders. The billow on one side of the kite will increase while the billow on the other side will decrease.

When the kite is hovering overhead, an unbalanced frame will give the illusion that the lines are not of equal length. You can demonstrate this effect by intentionally shifting your center spine connector about 1/2 inch.

Distortions can occur if the right and left side cross spars are not positioned at identical distances from their respective leading edge tips.

### REMEDY:

Always check the position of the center tee when you set up for a day of flying.

The top spreader connectors can be kept in place on most kites by gluing a short (1/4 inch) section of vinyl tubing to the leading edge spar just below the spreader connector. The bottom spreader connectors can be kept in place by gluing a short section of vinyl tubing to the leading edge spar just above the spreader connector. CAUTION: when you glue the piece of tubing above the leading edge connector for the bottom spreader, it will be difficult to remove the lower section of the leading edge spar. Because, of this, I use a RESTRAINING LINE to keep the bottom spreader connectors in place.

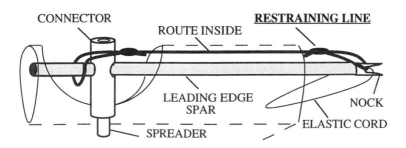

CONNECTOR  ROUTE INSIDE  RESTRAINING LINE
LEADING EDGE SPAR  NOCK
SPREADER  ELASTIC CORD

## CHECKING FOR EQUAL LENGTH LINES.

### STATIC METHOD:

1. Remove the lines from the kite.
2. Stake the kite ends of the lines firmly to the ground.
3. Pull on the handles with equal tension.
4. Compare the positions of the right and left handles. They should be exactly side by side.
5. Make the appropriate adjustment to the longer line.

### DYNAMIC METHOD:

The presentation of this method, in the Straight Line Flight section of this book, includes illustrations.

Fly the kite close to the ground, and then when the kite is just about to the center of the wind window, turn it to go straight up. Keep your hands close together. When the kite is going straight up in the center of the wind window, press your hands together tightly. This should be done when the kite is between 1/2 and 3/4 of the way up, and when the kite is still pulling. For best results, the pull should be moderate. Do not wait until the kite reaches the top, because if the kite were not in the center of the wind window it would start to turn. The kite will continue to go up to the top and hover. Determine which fly line is longer by examining the relative position of your hands. Do this test several times until the error is consistent. Then land the kite and make the appropriate adjustment to the length of the longer line.

# 26 ZIP-A-DEE DOO-DAH

This routine demonstrates the use of the entire wind window. It includes a variety of maneuvers which flow together. The diagrams are not drawn to scale and should be used as a general reference for size and approximate position in the wind window.

The choreography of this routine is matched to the Disney song **"Zip-A-Dee-Doo-Dah."** You will find the song on Volume One of The Disney Collection, compact disc number CD-002, DIDX 1756. The soundtrack only lasts for 2 minutes and 16 seconds. I needed a routine for competition that would last at least 3 minutes. Therefore, I found a convenient location to cut the music, which allowed me to replay some of the previous sections. If you choose to fly this routine to the music, you have two options.

First, use the music as is. Compare the patterns of diagrams 3 and 9 at the word, "SHOULDER." In diagram 3, shift the downward vertical path to the center of the wind window. Then, move directly from diagram 3 to diagram 9 to finish the short program.

Second, cut and splice the music. When recording your music for the longer program, let the music flow through to the word "SHOULDER" in diagram 9. Stop or Pause the recording tape immediately after the word "SHOULDER." Backtrack the disc and restart the recording tape immediately after the word "SHOULDER" in diagram 3. CAUTION; be careful not to restart the recording tape after the word "SHOULDER" in diagram 2.

*"I hope you enjoy this routine as much as I have."*

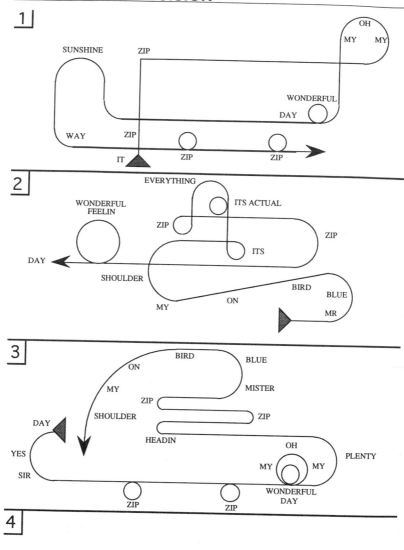

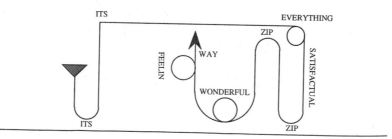

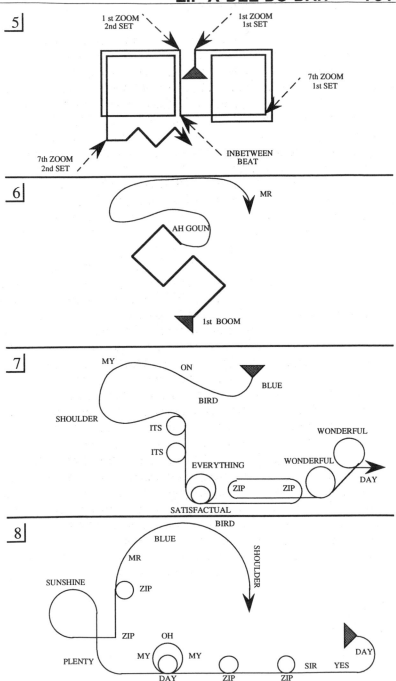

5 1st ZOOM 2nd SET 1st ZOOM 1st SET 7th ZOOM 1st SET 7th ZOOM 2nd SET INBETWEEN BEAT

6 MR AH GOUN 1st BOOM

7 MY ON BLUE BIRD SHOULDER ITS ITS EVERYTHING WONDERFUL WONDERFUL ZIP ZIP DAY SATISFACTUAL

8 BIRD BLUE SHOULDER MR SUNSHINE ZIP ZIP OH MY MY DAY PLENTY DAY ZIP ZIP SIR YES

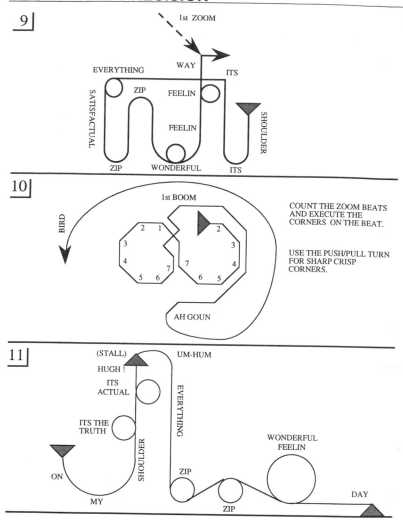

When flying this routine to the music, compensate for strong wind conditions by making the circles larger. When the winds are light, use shorter length fly lines. I usually use 75 to 100 foot lines on a six foot delta kite.

# 27 CHARIOTS OF FIRE

## CHOREOGRAPHED PAIRS ROUTINE

This routine is presented here as an introduction to the concept of two people flying a synchronized routine with their controllable kites. The diagrams are not drawn to scale and should only be used as a general reference for size and approximate position in the wind window.

The choreography of this routine is matched to the song **"Chariots Of Fire,"** track number 10 on the K-TEL compact disc number NU 1663, titled "Hooked On Themes." Learn to fly the patterns with your kite first, and then learn to match the patterns to the music.

I am currently writing a book that describes in detail the process of choreographing routines to music. However, I wanted to share a couple of introductory routines in this book. A dilemma almost kept me from including these routines. How could I tell you about matching the diagrams to the music without going into all of the technical aspects of dissecting the music into all of its parts? My conclusion was to provide you with approximate time marks along the diagrams as references. Most compact disc players have time counters that are within a few seconds of each other.

Study each diagram and take note of the time marks. Listen to the music keeping a particular time mark and pattern in mind. As the time mark appears, you will hear the music that is meant to match that pattern. Take a quick glance at the diagram for the next pattern and time mark. Then, watch the counter again.

If you don't have a partner to fly with, fly either the leader or the follower part by itself. On the other hand, you could fly 2 kites at the same time and do both parts yourself.

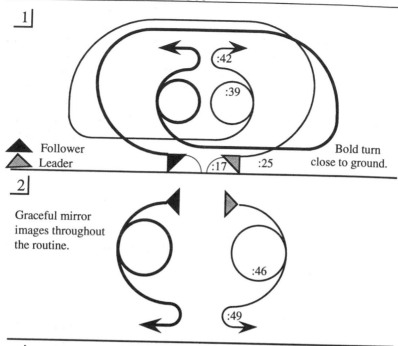

**1**

Follower
Leader

:42
:39
:17    :25

Bold turn close to ground.

**2**

Graceful mirror images throughout the routine.

:46
:49

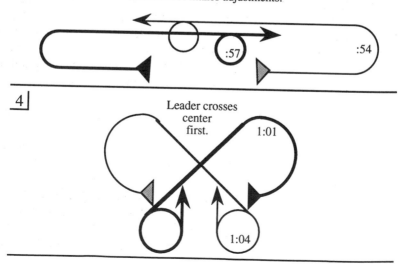

**3**

Straight horizontal lines.

Pass as close as possible.
The leader flys straight and
the follower makes adjustments.

:57      :54

**4**

Leader crosses center first.

1:01
1:04

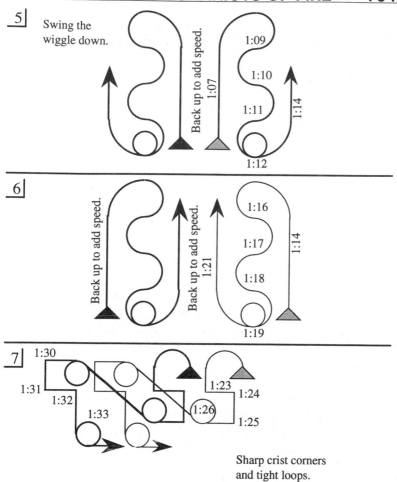

**5** Swing the wiggle down.

Back up to add speed.
1:07

1:09
1:10
1:11
1:12
1:14

**6** Back up to add speed.

Back up to add speed.
1:21

1:16
1:17
1:18
1:19
1:14

**7** 1:30
1:31
1:32
1:33
1:23
1:24
1:25
1:26

Sharp crist corners
and tight loops.

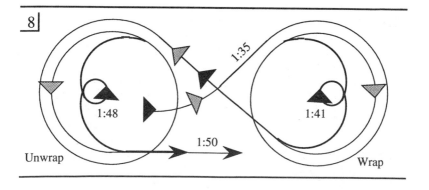

**8**
1:35
1:48
1:41
1:50
Unwrap
Wrap

9|

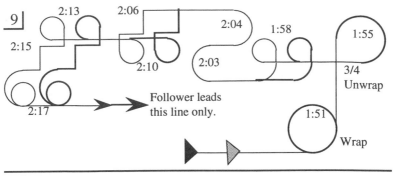

2:13  2:06  2:04  1:58  1:55
2:15
2:10  2:03  3/4 Unwrap
2:17  Follower leads this line only.
1:51  Wrap

10|

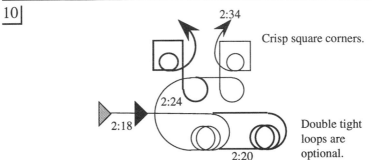

2:34  Crisp square corners.
2:24
2:18
Double tight loops are optional.
2:20

11|

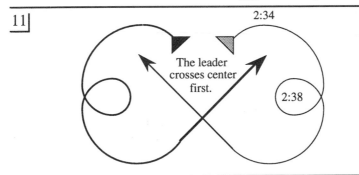

2:34
The leader crosses center first.
2:38

12|

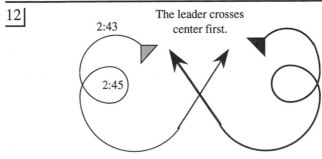

The leader crosses center first.
2:43
2:45

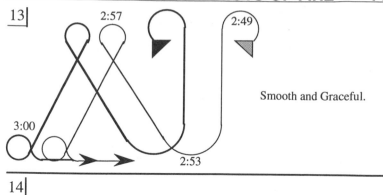

13

2:57

2:49

3:00

2:53

Smooth and Graceful.

14

Walk toward the kites to slow them down.
Make larger circles in stronger wind.

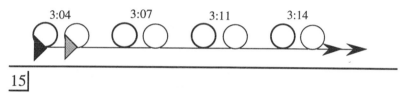

3:04        3:07        3:11        3:14

15

Loop and land to end
the routine.

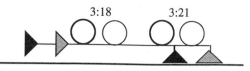

3:18        3:21

*A kite routine choreographed to music is
an Artistic Interpretation of an Artistic Composition.*

# *28* 3-PERSON TEAM

Here are a few 3-person team stunts that illustrate "Preparatory" and "Execution" commands. A sequence of team maneuvers is used to present a specific picture in the sky. This picture is given a name that becomes the "Preparatory" command of the stunt. The leader calls out the "Preparatory" command to tell the team members the next picture. A total picture may contain several separate elements. The flyers will execute their separate elements, when the leader calls out the "Execution" commands. The end result will be a synchronized presentation of the picture.

This first stunt represents a Water Fountain and the "Preparatory" command is "FOUNTAIN." The "Execution" command, "TURN," will start each of the 5 elements in this stunt.

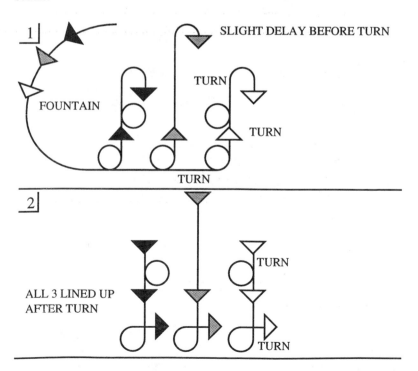

The second stunt represents a Boomerang being thrown into the sky and then being caught as it comes down. The "Preparatory" command is "BOOMERANG." The "Execution" command, "TURN," will start each of the 3 elements in this stunt and one additional element to clear the overlapped lines.

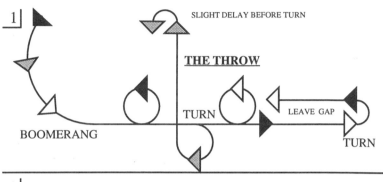

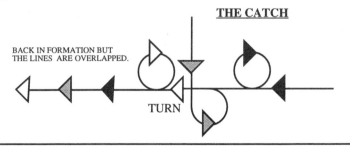

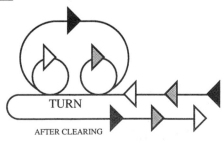

# RAZZLE DAZZLE

This stunt consists of 5 consecutive threads with the needle indexing 90 degrees clockwise each time. Pay particular attention to the order of passage of the two crossing kites in diagrams 2, 3, and 5. The diagrams imply which kite is to go first. Do the stunt as tightly as you can for effect.

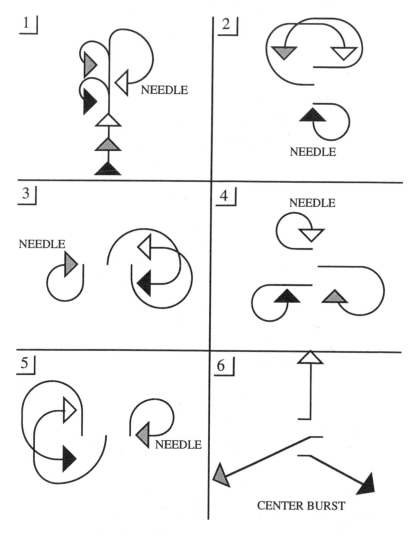

# ROBIN HOOD

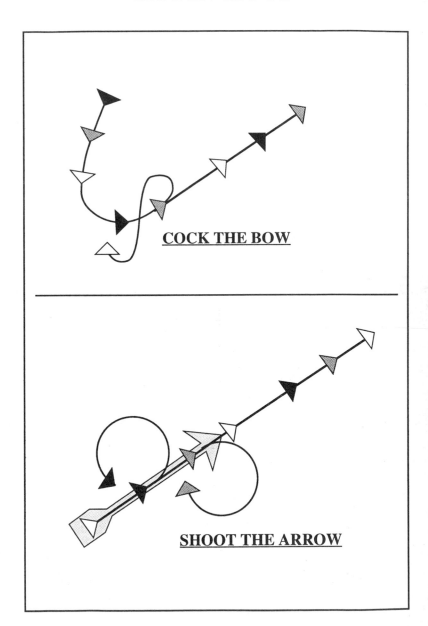

**COCK THE BOW**

**SHOOT THE ARROW**

# *29* THE GREATEST LOVE OF ALL

## CHOREOGRAPHED 4-PERSON ROUTINE

This routine is presented here as an introduction to the concept of four persons flying a synchronized routine with their controllable kites. The diagrams are not drawn to scale and should only be used as a general reference for size and approximate position in the wind window.

The choreography of this routine is matched to the song, **"The Greatest Love Of All,"** track number 15 on the K-TEL compact disc, number NU 1663, titled, "Hooked On Themes." Learn to fly the patterns with your kites first, and then learn to match the patterns to the music.

I have provided you with approximate time marks along the diagrams as references. Most compact disc players have time counters that are within a few seconds of each other. Listen carefully to the music while observing the appropriate patterns. You will get a feeling of the way that the patterns are relating to the music.

Each kite is represented by a specific image. Each kite's image is shown at the beginning and the end of each diagram. Each subsequent diagram continues from where the previous diagram ended. Complete sets of the 4 different images are shown the same number of times in a diagram. Each of these sets represents a check mark for each kite at that moment in the routine.

△ 1 The Leader

◮ 2 First Follower

◣ 3 Alternate Leader

◢ 4 Tail Gunner

The Leader will stand to the right of the group and give the commands.

The Alternate Leader is in charge of one side during the mirror image maneuvers.

Here are some suggested preparatory commands:

| COMMAND | DIAGRAM |
|---|---|
| BRACKET-RIGHT | 1 and 2 |
| LEFT-OBLIQUE | 3 |
| RIGHT | 3 |
| 3/4-LEFT | 3 |
| SWEEP-TO-THE-EDGE | 3 |
| FIGURE-8-SERIES | 4, 5, 6, 7, 8, 9 |
| DOUGHNUT-THREAD | 10, 11, 12 |
| BARREL-ROLL-THREAD | 13, 14, 15, 16 |
| HESITATION-STAR-BURST | 17,18 |
| BUMP-SERIES | 19, 20 |
| FIGURE-EIGHTS | 21, 22 |
| SQUARES | 23, 24 |
| SWOOP | 25 |
| LITTLE-SQUARE-LEFT | 25 |
| RIGHT | 25 |
| PEEL-OFF-TO-WEAVE | 26 |
| WEAVE | 27 |
| ODD-EVEN-LEFT | 28 |
| SWEEP-TO-THE-EDGE | 29 |
| LANDING-SERIES | 30, 31, 32, 33 |

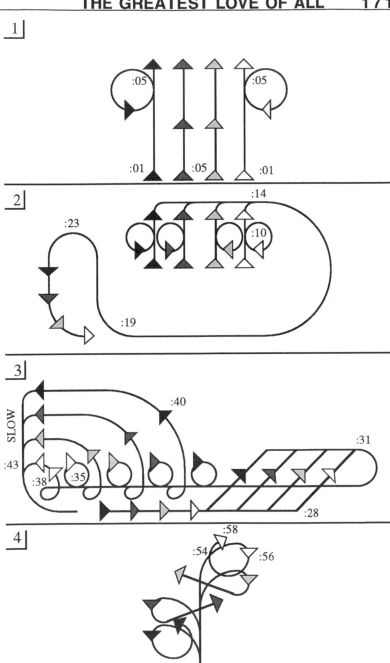

5|                           :58

6|            1:02

7|     1:05

8|                    1:11

9|                              1:15

10|          1:23

              1:27

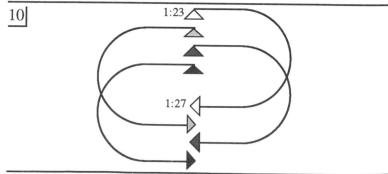

11|

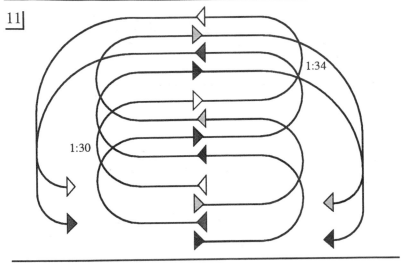

1:34

1:30

12|

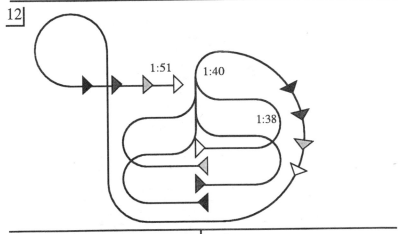

1:51 1:40

1:38

13|

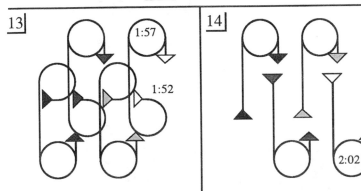

1:57

1:52

14|

2:02

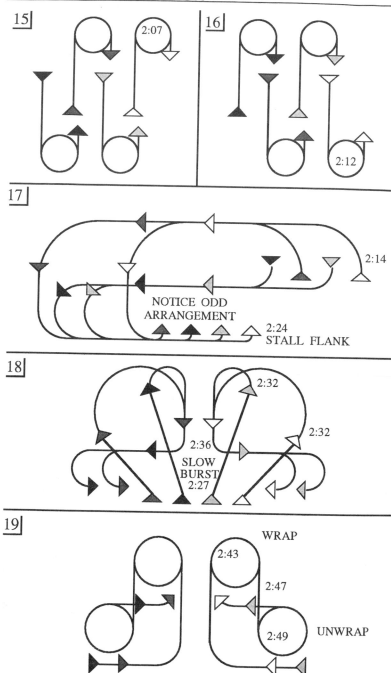

15

2:07

16

2:12

17

2:14

NOTICE ODD
ARRANGEMENT

2:24
STALL  FLANK

18

2:32

2:32

2:36

SLOW
BURST
2:27

19

WRAP

2:43

2:47

2:49   UNWRAP

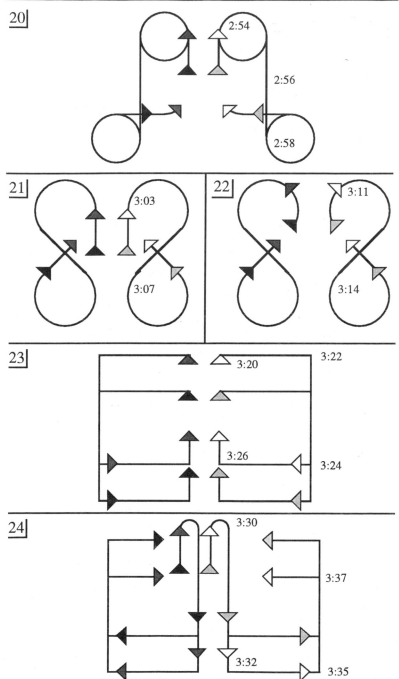

25|

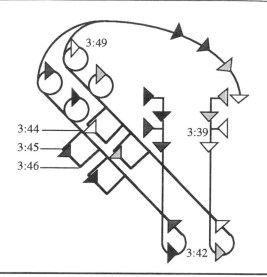

3:49

3:44

3:45

3:46

3:39

3:42

26|

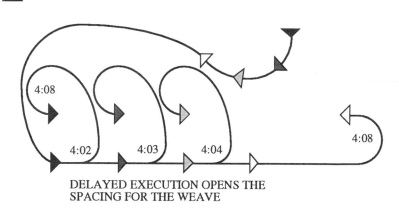

4:08

4:02    4:03    4:04

4:08

DELAYED EXECUTION OPENS THE
SPACING FOR THE WEAVE

27|

4:15

4:11

4:15

28|

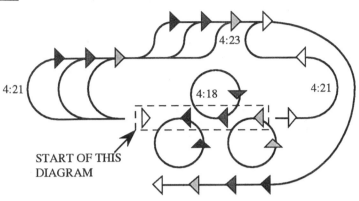

4:23

4:21

4:18

4:21

START OF THIS
DIAGRAM

29|

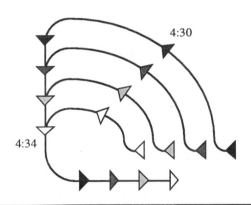

4:30

4:34

30|

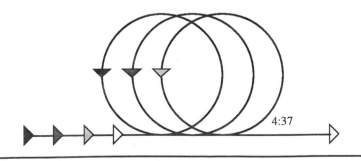

4:37

31|

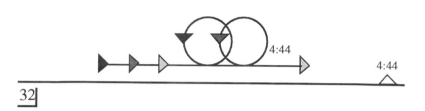

32|

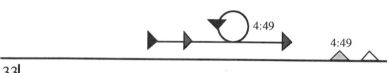

33|

This routine was flown extensively in National Competition and International Demonstrations from Mar., 1989 through Sept., 1992. It won the American Grand National Team Ballet event in Oct., 1989. Initially, it was flown with single 8 ft. delta kites. Later, it was flown with trains of six (6-ft. delta) kites. Ultimately, the team members were taking their Execution cues directly from the notes of the music. That is the most enjoyable way to experience team ballet.

# GLOSSARY

**Billow:** The pocket created by the sail set back away from the frame.

**Cellular:** Fabric pockets that inflate with the wind.

**Center of the Wind Window:** The flier's line of sight in the direction that the wind is blowing.

**Compulsory Figures:** Required geometric patterns flown in competition.

**Control Bar:** A strong handle with the right and left fly lines attached to opposite ends, thereby allownming the flyer to control the kite with one hand.

**Down Wind:** In the same direction that the wind is blowing.

**Edge of the Wind Window:** The point of transition between down-wind and up-wind.

**Edge Work:** Maneuvers of the kite at the edge of the wind window.

**Execution Command:** A short word spoken by the leader of a team to indicate the point at which a control action is to take place.

**False Wrap:** When both ends are held stationary and the lines are revolved around each other at the center.

**Follow The Leader:** Two or more kites flying in formation, whereby one kite becomes the leader and the other kites follow in its path.

**Framed Kites:** Ones that contain spars to establish their shape.

**Geometric Figure:** Circles, Squares, Triangles...etc. presented as a path for the kite to fly.

**Ground Pass:** The path of the kite parallel to the ground.

**Ground Work:** Maneuvers of the kite involving contact with the ground.

**Hollow Braided:** A string with a tubular weave and no center core.

**Horizontal Thread:** Kites on a horizontal path that pass eachother in opposite directions. Usually one kite will pass between two others.

**Launch:** The kite leaves the ground--Takeoff.

**Locked Up:** The condition of the lines will not allow the flyer to steer the kite. False wraps and excessive twists will create this condition.

**Mirror Image Maneuver:** Kites fly reversed patterns on opposite sides of an imaginary centerline.

**Pre-sleeved:** String provided by the manufacturer with a protective jacket over both ends.

**Pre-stretched:** String that has been stretched by the manufacturer to tighten the weave.

**Preparatory Command:** A name assigned to a series of maneuvers to be flown by a team.

**Sail Positioner:** A small rod used to push the sail away from the bottom spreader.

**Sleeving:** A protective jacket at the ends of the string.

**Soft Kites:** Their shape is established by the wind pressure. They do not contain any spars.

**Tied to Length:** To make up a line to a specific measurement.

**Top of the Wind Window:** The highest point to which the kite will climb.

**Train Lines:** Short equal length lines used to attach one kite behind another to create a train.

**Train:** Two or more kites attached together one behind the other.

**Twisted Lines:** The condition of a set of lines, when one end is held stationary while the other ends are revolved around each other.

**Vinyl Connector:** A short section of vinyl tubing used to connect the spars.

**Wind Window:** The total flying area of the sky. Looking down wind, the wind window will include all the down wind area extending from ground level on your extreme left in an arc up over the top of your head and down to ground level on your extreme right.

**Wing-Tip Turn:** A tight turn with the wing tip at the center of the radius.

# INDEX

*No Wind Too Light
No Line Too Tight*

# Order Form

**KITE PRECISION**     **by Ron Reich**

Ship To:

Name: _____

Address: _____

City: _____ State: _____

           Zip Code: _____ - _____

Phone Number:    (    ) _____

Number of books ordered:_____ @$14.95ea  =    $ _____

**Book Rate Shipping:** Allow 3 to 4 Weeks Delivery.

Shipping first book: _____$2.50_____ Sub Total: ____$ _____

Shipping ea additional book: $0.75 _____ Sub Total: ____$ _____

**Air Mail Shipping:** $3.50 per book x _____books = $_____

Sales Tax:
Please add 7.75% for books shipped to California addresses.   $ _____

                                 Total    $ _____

Make Check or Money Order Payable To: TUTOR TEXT

Send Order To:          TUTOR TEXT
                     P.O. BOX 1605
                   RAMONA, CA, 92065-0895

Phone or Fax (619) 789-7780 for more information.